How to Stop Procrastinating

Powerful Strategies to Overcome Laziness and Multiply Your Time

Daniel Walter

HOW TO STOP PROCRASTINATING:
Powerful Strategies to Overcome Laziness
and Multiply Your Time
by Daniel Walter

© Copyright 2020 by Daniel Walter

All Rights Reserved.

Disclaimer: This book is designed to provide accurate and authoritative information in regard to the subject matter covered. By its sale, neither the publisher nor the author is engaged in rendering psychological or other professional services. If expert assistance or counseling is needed, the services of a competent professional should be sought.

ISBN: 979-8706661441

ALSO BY DANIEL WALTER

The Power of Discipline:
How to Use Self Control and Mental Toughness
to Achieve Your Goals

CONTENTS

INTRODUCTION

The word procrastination originates from two Latin words—"pro," which means "for" and "cras," which means "tomorrow." The literal translation of these words is "to leave something for tomorrow." In other words, procrastination is postponing the things we know we should do now. And if you are guilty of procrastination, we all know that it doesn't mean just until tomorrow! When I was stuck in the procrastination rut, I had things on my to-do list for years!

Procrastination is the opposite of productivity. To produce, we've got to take action so that we can push things forward. When we procrastinate, we push things back to tomorrow, next week, and in some cases—never. Procrastination is a disease of the psyche that prevents people from reaching their highest potential in life.

People who are content with mediocrity make jokes about procrastination, but when you get serious about life and realize that it is a severe hindrance to your progress, you will start making changes. That's what happened to me; I have always wanted to be an author. I had written out the outline for my first book several years before it was published, but anytime I sat down to write it, I found myself indulging in every distraction and temptation possible—I just couldn't get focused.

As soon as I learned how to overcome procrastination, the sky was the limit for me! I am now at the top of my game, living the life of my dreams—a life that I once believed was only available to the "lucky ones." I had no idea how much power I had over my future. I would look at people like Bill Gates, Steve Jobs, and Oprah Winfrey and assume they had some special gene that propelled them into greatness. But I have learned that one of the ingredients for success is eliminating procrastination from your life.

We all have 24 hours in a day to get things done, so why is it that some people manage to achieve more than others? They accomplish things because they don't waste time on unproductive activities that hinder their progress. You are probably one of the many people who make statements like, *"There just aren't enough hours in the day."* If Bill Gates and Warren Buffet can become two of the richest men on the planet using the same 24 hours a day that we all have, then it's not that they are some extraterrestrial angelic beings, but that we waste the time that we have been given.

When I stopped procrastinating, several things started to happen, and I believe you will experience them too, once you begin to apply the principles I have outlined in this book.

- You will feel relaxed and free—no more feelings of worthlessness and guilt for not getting things done.
- You will become more productive and effective.
- You will start following your dreams.
- You will start keeping important commitments.
- When you start achieving your goals, that success will boost your self-esteem.

You will find that overcoming procrastination will set you on a path you had no idea was always there waiting for you to explore. This book will enlighten your mind and open your eyes to the infinite possibilities that are available to you, if only you are willing to put in the hard work. Achieving your core goals is dependent upon your ability to overcome procrastination, whether you want more financial freedom, happiness, or personal fulfillment—whatever you want out of life—this book will act as your guide by helping you overcome procrastination.

The time is now, not tomorrow, not next week. Don't waste another day—now is the time for transformation. Life doesn't give you anything. You've got to take it, and unless you get up and go after it, you will never attain what you want!

Dive deep into these eleven powerful chapters, put knowledge into action, stop procrastinating, and start living the purposeful life you were destined for.

JOIN OUR PRODUCTIVITY GROUP

To maximize the value you receive from this book, I highly encourage you to join our tight-knit community on Facebook. Here you will be able to connect and share strategies for overcoming procrastination to continue your growth.

Taking this journey alone is not recommended, and this can be an excellent support network for you.

It would be great to connect with you there,

Daniel Walter

To Join, Visit:
www.pristinepublish.com/focusgroup

DOWNLOAD THE AUDIO VERSION OF THIS BOOK FREE

If you love listening to audiobooks on the go or would enjoy a narration as you read along, I have great news for you. You can download the audio book version of *How to Stop Procrastinating* for FREE (Regularly $14.95) just by signing up for a FREE 30-day audible trial!

Visit: www.pristinepublish.com/audiobooks

YOUR FREE GIFT -
MASTER YOUR MORNING

Just thinking about the word "morning" can put a bad taste in people's mouths. A recent study found that one in four Americans hit the snooze button twice before getting out of bed. Forty-nine percent of the same sample stated that waking up late is the main reason they are always late.

In other words, too many of us struggle with productivity, and there are very few people who jump out of bed as soon as their alarm goes off, excited about starting the day.

I want you to take a couple of minutes and think about what your morning usually looks like…

So you don't feel alone in this, I'll start with what mine looked like a little less than three years ago.

- Set my alarm for 6am, hit the snooze button until 7am
- Jump out of bed, shower, get dressed and run out the door
- Get a McDonalds breakfast and eat it on my way to work
- Shout at the drivers on the road because it's their fault I woke up an hour late
- Get to work with two minutes to spare
- Sit at my desk stuffing my face with coffee and snacks all morning to keep my energy levels up

But then I learned about the power of a consistent morning routine and my life changed. I went from thinking I'd never achieve my dreams, to seeing them slowly manifest while I was becoming confident that I could have anything I set my mind to. Let me start by explaining how healthy morning routines are created and why they make us more productive.

If I had to use an alternative word for "routine," I'd use the word "freedom" because that's what it gives us. Think about it like this: what's the first thing you do when you wake up in the morning? Most of you are going to say, "Brush my teeth." That's because it's a habit. Since childhood, we've been trained to brush our teeth as soon as we get out of bed in the morning, so we don't even think about it, we just do it. When you get in your car every morning to go to work, do you sit there thinking about how you're going to drive your vehicle? No, you just put your foot on the accelerator and go because it's a habit. But when you were first learning to drive, your driving instructor had to tell you what to do, and you had to think carefully about it when you were on the road. It may have taken a while, but you got there in the end, didn't you?

Establishing a morning routine works in the same way. Once it becomes a habit, and you're powering through your routine on autopilot, it will give you freedom because you will no longer struggle to succeed.

When we get down to basics, routines are the foundation of life; everything you do is routine, even if you don't think it is. Your bad morning habits of getting up late and having breakfast on the go have become a routine. The way you style your hair is a routine, the location you leave your shoes when you return home is a routine. Can you see my point? Everything is about routine.

The problem is that your current routines aren't doing you any favors. In fact, they're hindering you. Everything you do in the morning has become an enemy of progress, and the longer you continue living this way, the longer your success will be delayed. If you're anything like me, you probably don't know where to start when it comes to establishing a morning routine. I had no idea what I was doing when I started on this journey, but I had some good people in my life who gave me step-by-step instructions, and now I want to give them to you.

In my bonus e-book, *Master Your Morning,* you will learn about the seven habits you need to apply to become that person who jumps out of bed every morning raring to go. Here are three of them:

1. **A Bedtime Routine:** Sleep is one of the most important things you'll do every evening. Sleep is wonderful, we all love sleeping, which is the main reason why so many of you hit the snooze button every morning! You've probably heard that healthy adults need eight hours of sleep a night, right? Arguably, this is true, but what you may not know is that the quality of your sleep is more important than the quantity. Do you wake up feeling drained and tired no matter how many hours of sleep you get? That's because you're not getting good-quality sleep. And the reason is that you've got a terrible night-time routine.

2. **Wake up early:** As you've just read, it's the quality of your sleep that will determine whether you wake up refreshed or not. The first step to dropping the terrible habit of smashing the snooze button every morning is establishing a good bedtime routine so you wake up

feeling refreshed and energized. Waking up early is an essential habit to cultivate if you want to succeed because it gives you a head start on the day.

3. **No Electronics:** Did you know that smartphone addiction is a real thing? I was addicted to my phone, and I had zero awareness of it. Every time it pinged, I would check to see who was messaging me, and I was always on social media. If you're going to get anywhere in life, kicking this habit is essential, and I'll show you how to do it.

Just by pondering these three habits, can you see where you're going wrong? That's just a snippet of what's in store for you in *Master Your Morning*. You will have access to an abundance of helpful information that will kickstart your journey toward success and get you one step closer to living your dream life.

If you've got to that point where you're sick and tired of being sick and tired, this book is for you. It will equip you with everything you need to become more productive and start taking control of your life instead of letting life control you!

Get *Master Your Morning* for Free by Visiting

www.pristinepublish.com/morningbonus

CHAPTER 1:

THE COMPONENTS OF PROCRASTINATION

Janet has always thought about starting her own business. She has been stuck at a dead-end job for the past five years, and she is constantly fantasizing about the day when she won't have to report to her micro-managing boss, deal with mounds of mind-numbing paperwork, or leave her 2-year-old daughter with a babysitter every morning. Her concern was that she didn't know of any other way to continue supporting herself and her family financially without the job she hated. After thinking long and hard about her situation, she decided that she would start her restaurant as a delivery service from home.

At first, it was nothing but a fantasy, something she day-dreamed about to get herself through the day; but one day, something clicked, and she decided to take action. After all, cooking was her passion. She had been cooking for friends and family for years, and they were so impressed with her skills that they were always telling her to open her own restaurant. So Janet decided that she was going to give it a try, but there was no way she could afford to quit her job, so she took a two-week vacation to get started.

Her first step was research. She needed to understand the business side of things before she could get going. Janet was going to find out everything she needed to know about finance management, taxes, and recipes. She also planned on doing market research in her town to find out the wants, needs, and desires of her target audience.

Unfortunately, all of Janet's ideas took form in her head and stayed there! The thought of having to learn everything from scratch was so overwhelming that it paralyzed her from taking action. Leases, business filings, and taxes did not appeal to her—all she wanted to do was cook! Once her vacation started, she would find anything else to do other than the things she had initially planned. She spent her days playing with her daughter, sleeping in, doing housework, visiting friends, and gossiping with neighbors but failing to ask any questions about her market research project.

Two weeks came and went, and she had achieved nothing! As Janet made her way to work, the thought of opening her own restaurant continued to remain at the top of her mind, and that's exactly where it stayed—in her mind.

WHY DID JANET PROCRASTINATE?

What do you think went wrong in Janet's situation? Did she lack persistence, focus, action, or self-discipline? She lacked all of the above, and combined, they amount to procrastination. This is a classic case of procrastination manifesting as a dream killer. If you are going to achieve anything, you must have the ability to follow through, and if you are lacking in any of these components, you will have a difficult time overcoming this negative habit. I refer to each component as a body part so that you can fully comprehend how important they are:

Focus – The Head: Your ability to follow through will determine your ability to focus. It is focus that keeps your head in the right direction and your eyes on the prize. Focus is like the rudder that steers your thoughts and guides your actions toward turning your vision into reality. There is more to following through than putting in enough effort—it's about targeting your effort towards a single goal. With focus, your efforts will never go to waste. You operate through tunnel vision so that everything you do is directed toward your end goal.

Looking back at Janet's situation, if she had been focused on starting her business, she would have spent those two weeks doing the things that were required to bring that vision to life.

Self-Discipline – The Spine: When someone breaks their spine, it cripples the entire body. When it comes to overcoming procrastination, you need a strong "backbone," so therefore, self-discipline is the most important trait. Self-discipline enables you to do the things that need to be done even when you don't feel like it. It's the ability to control yourself so that you can maintain your focus and power through important tasks essential to achieving your goals regardless of distractions or temptations. Self-discipline is essential to over-coming procrastination because it gives you the strength to regulate your actions, thoughts, and feelings. Without self-discipline, you wouldn't have the ability to put consistent effort into your work.

As the head is connected to the spine, focus is connected to self-discipline. Focus will give you the self-discipline you need to follow through. Similarly, if you are self-disciplined, you will find it easy to focus, avoid distractions, and work on what needs to be done. Like the spine, self-discipline keeps the body erect so that you don't fall into disorder.

If Janet had enough self-discipline, she would have restrained herself from using all her free time to indulge in leisure activities. There is nothing wrong with getting together with loved ones or catching up on needed sleep. However, if you spend the majority of your time doing this and it affects your productivity, then you have a problem. Leisure in moderation is just as important to success as hard work; nevertheless, it can become a vice when it isn't used properly.

Action – The Hands and Feet: To overcome procrastination, you must prioritize execution, and you must be intentional about the things you want to achieve. This means you must hit the ground running every day. It is action that will get you from point A to point B so that your dreams become tangible and not just a vision in your head. Without action, you wouldn't be able to measure your progress and your dreams will remain dreams. It is also important to realize that it's not about taking massive action. One of the things that overwhelmed Janet was the total amount of work she had to do to get to her final destination. But if she had broken her goals down into manageable chunks—for example, Monday through Friday spend 1 hour in the morning, afternoon, and evening reading about taxes—she would have been one real step closer to realizing her dream. Action breeds momentum; once you get going, you won't want to stop.

Persistence – The Heart: And last but not least, the heart of following through is persistence. Persistence is refusing to give up on something even when it appears that it isn't working and there are many obstacles on your path. Persistence is the tenacity to leap over hurdles no matter how high they appear. Starting something is great, but it's getting to the finish line that matters.

You must have a strong heart to do this because obstacles are challenging, and the majority of people give up when they encounter them.

Did Janet have the persistence to follow through? I can't answer that question because you can measure persistence only when a person starts something and challenges arise, but Janet didn't get started.

CHAPTER 2:

WHY DO WE PROCRASTINATE?

When it comes to thinking about what we need to do, what we want to do, and what other people should be doing, we are experts. Our creative juices begin to flow, we come up with a complete mental blueprint, and we envision a clear picture of the life of our dreams. But when it comes to getting off our backsides and actually doing the work to turn this vision into a reality, we suddenly become disabled, and we lack the self-discipline, focus, action, and persistence required to get the job done.

There are times when we try to take on the challenge without our heads or our spines; other times, it's our hands or feet. You would assume we could just get these parts to work when we need them to, but the reality is that it's never that simple.

The enthusiasm and excitement with which we thought out our plans and dreams are gone with the wind as soon as we realize the gut-wrenching hard work it will take to bring those plans to life and turn those dreams into a reality. As a result, we don't follow through, and it's not because we lack the ability or intelligence. There are two main reasons we find it difficult to follow through with what we started: inhibiting tactics and psychological barriers.

INHIBITING TACTICS

Inhibiting tactics describe the excuses we make for misusing the time we've been given. Whether consciously or unconsciously, we engage in self-sabotaging behaviors that prevent us from moving forward. These tactics include:

- Setting the wrong goals
- Poor time management
- Engaging in distractions or temptations

Setting the Wrong Goals: Goals are necessary if you are going to achieve your dreams. However, when you set goals that are too difficult or too abstract, you set yourself up for failure. You can compare setting the wrong goals to putting the wrong zip code into a GPS—you will never arrive at your destination. In the same way, you will never arrive at your destination with the wrong goals. When you are running around in circles, you will lose patience eventually and give up.

Abstract goals are just as bad. This is the situation when we don't know what needs to be done to achieve our goals. For example, let's say you want to improve your health, but you haven't defined what it means to be healthy. You are less likely to work toward accomplishing anything. You might have the desire to be healthy, but because you don't know what to do, you never achieve it.

When our goals are too unrealistic or too high for any mortal to reach, we find ourselves staring up at a giant ladder without any rungs. I am not saying you shouldn't be ambitious; I believe you should shoot for the stars—"aim high" is my motto, and if you miss and hit the moon instead, that's still quite an accomplishment. However, an unrealistic goal is something like, *"I am going to lose 100 pounds in a week."* Really? When you set unrealistic goals, you almost know you are never going to achieve them; after all, how can you chastise someone for their inability to climb a ladder with no rungs?

Poor Time Management: We all have 24 hours in a day, and what we choose to do with that time will determine whether we get the things on our to-do list done or not. Unfortunately, too many of us waste time on pointless, random activities and then claim that there are not enough hours in the day to get things done.

Time management involves using time in a way that maximizes efficiency and productivity. Good time management means you are capable of scheduling tasks, exercising good judgment, and developing the insight to recognize when to do them. Additionally, it involves having the self-discipline to carry out those tasks as you had planned, and the focus to ensure that you have your resources organized accordingly. With good time management, a schedule is strategically organized and swiftly followed through on, so that tasks are completed as planned.

Poor time management, on the other hand, involves a lack of self-discipline, planning, focus, or organization. We underestimate how long projects will take to complete, and important deadlines are overlooked. Poor time management leads to a domino effect that hinders the rest of our plans. We fail to prepare for the future and prioritize our activities, which leads to cancelations and delays. Instead, we engage in non-essential tasks that have no real end goal.

There is no doubt that life today is challenging, and it is even more difficult than ever to maintain a healthy work-life balance. Not only has technology provided more opportunities, but it is also a major source of distraction, and 24 hours never seems enough to do the things we need to do. So bad time management has become the norm and good time management is a superpower that only the enlightened few have mastered. If we find it difficult to manage day-to-day tasks, how can we expect to manage our time to achieve our life's goals?

Engaging in Distractions or Temptations: The road to goal attainment would be easy enough to travel if there were no delays; if the road was straight and we could walk along it with no hindrances. If we had nothing to do other than work toward our goals, that's probably what we would do. Unfortunately, that is not the case. The road is lined with inviting rest stops, glittery detour signs, and a host of other shiny objects. Distractions and temptations come aplenty these days, from our phones to Netflix to computer games, there is always something more appealing to do than work.

However, it is impossible to rid the world of distractions and temptations. The problem isn't the temptations and distractions, but that we lack the ability to handle them. We can manage them through moderate, healthy use patterns, and strategic avoidance, however.

First, what is it that distracts and tempts you? For example, if you find it difficult to ignore messages when they appear, you can shut off your notifications while you work. Second, there is no need to deprive yourself completely of these things. The key is to use them in moderation. It is necessary to take a break from stressful work-related activities; that allows us to recharge our batteries so we can maximize our productivity. So, you might work until lunchtime, and then during your break dedicate a few minutes to catching up on messages, watching videos, or whatever else you enjoy.

PSYCHOLOGICAL ROADBLOCKS

Psychological roadblocks are the unconscious, internal mechanisms that act us barricades to our success. They work internally, preventing us from taking external action:

- A lack of self-awareness
- Perfectionism due to insecurity
- Laziness and a lack of discipline
- A fear of failure, rejection, and judgment

A Lack of Self-Awareness: When we are so fearful of leaving our comfort zone because we might make a mistake, we never reach our full potential. As a result, many of our passions and interests remain hidden from the world. You will never know what you are capable of unless you try; and therefore, you remain convinced that you are incapable and you never follow through on your plans. You then become trapped in a lifetime of stagnation. Additionally, we don't realize that stagnation has become our downfall because we are not aware that we are not following through. We go on with our lives believing that there is nothing else we can do to work harder than we already are. However, if we were to remove the unnecessary distractions from our lives and take some time out to look at the bigger picture, it would open our eyes to the reality that what we have been doing all along is avoiding doing what is required to achieve our goals.

Perfectionism Due to Insecurity: Jason has been thinking about applying for a promotion for years. He has been working to upgrade his skills and professional knowledge, enrolling in postgraduate classes, taking certification exams, and attending seminars. He aims to create a perfect resume so that he can be confident he will get the promotion when he applies. For Jason, if it wasn't perfect, he wouldn't take action until it was.

Despite all his efforts, two years went by and he still hadn't applied for the promotion because he didn't think he had gained enough credentials. His perfectionism was rooted in his deep insecurity and fear that he wasn't good enough, which prevented Jason from taking action. All his energy was focused on striving for perfection and over planning, which ultimately led to stagnation. From the outside looking in, it would appear that Jason was a go-getter working toward his goals; but in reality, all his efforts were really going into avoiding applying for the promotion.

Laziness and a Lack of Discipline: Sometimes, laziness and a lack of discipline will prevent us from following through. When you hit the snooze button despite having had eight hours of sleep, lie on the couch flicking through channels, or spend hours talking on the phone even though you know you've got work to do, you only have yourself to blame when you are unable to complete important tasks in a timely manner. A lack of discipline causes you to waste time on distractions and temptations and you do not have enough willpower to either get started or to continue what you have started. When you think about the sacrifices required to get things done, whether consciously or unconsciously, you decide that it's not worth it.

Our bodies are activated to move through willpower, while discipline is the focus that directs our willpower to move toward our goals. When willpower and discipline are absent, we remain in a state of inactivity and fail to follow through.

A Fear of Failure, Rejection, and Judgment: Sabrina is a volunteer for a local organization that provides education for underprivileged children. She has come up with a fundraising campaign idea that will attract more sponsors. Sabrina has thought about the research she needs to do and the people she needs to call to get things moving. But before she dials the first number, she stops and thinks about all the things that could go wrong if she organizes the campaign. *"What if I get the support I need from community leaders, but no one shows up? What if we end up spending more money than we make? What if no one is interested in the campaign?"* After spending some time answering her own questions, she decides to abandon the idea and immediately feels better for doing so.

Sabrina didn't follow through because she was afraid of failure, rejection, and judgment. In her mind, deciding not to take action was an act of self-preservation. It was her way of protecting herself from the pain of failure. She couldn't get rejected because she didn't ask for anything, and no one could say she failed because she didn't attempt to go after her goal.

The fear of failure, rejection, and judgment paralyzes us and stops us from working toward our goals. We think that by not taking action, we eliminate the possibility of doing something that might lead to negative judgment. If we don't attempt to do the things that challenge us, it's impossible to fail. However, you fail the moment you decide not to try.

So why not shift your perspective for a minute for the sake of your happiness and personal development. Think about what life would be like if you made it a habit to follow through on all of your goals.

What Happens When We Stop Procrastinating?

There is no denying the fact that going after what you want is difficult—it is easier to give up than to move forward with your dreams. However, the benefits associated with achieving your goals far outweigh the struggles we experience to get there. By developing a habit of following through, you will maximize opportunities, increase your productivity, and reach your full potential. Your career or academic goals will become realistic guideposts in life instead of just being pipedreams that frustrate you when you think about your inability to achieve them.

Success is not the only benefit of consistently following through. You will also gain the trust and respect of your friends, family members, and co-workers. As you learn to keep promises to yourself, that practice will extend to every other area of your life. You also will build better relationships with these people because they know they can trust you.

Additionally, you will establish a better relationship with yourself. Following through teaches you to get in touch with your own capacities, wants, needs, and fears on a deeper level so that you are in a better position to take control of your life instead of being a slave to your fears.

Following through is a powerful combination of persistence, action, self-discipline, and focus. It is the force that propels you toward greater personal satisfaction, better relationships, and higher achievements. However, as you have read, inhibiting tactics and psychological roadblocks can prevent you from consistently following through on your goals and dreams. You might start with the passion and motivation to do something, but as time goes on, the flame within you ceases to burn. To reignite it, you must first determine what's hindering you, and then equip yourself with the necessary tools to ensure that you are able to follow through on the things you have set out to do in the future.

Do you remember the story of Janet at the beginning of chapter one? She booked a two-week vacation to focus on establishing her business, but she returned to work failing to achieve any of the goals she had set for herself. She was unable to follow through because she allowed distractions, temptations, and the fear of failure to override what was most important to her. Living the life of her dreams required too much work, and she wasn't willing to make the sacrifice; therefore, she went back to a life of misery.

What if Janet was aware of the obstacles that were preventing her from following through? Suppose she fought back by using the right psychological tools and tactics to overcome these barriers and eventually succeeded in running her own restaurant. Instead of waking up depressed and not wanting to go to work, instead of living for Fridays and hating Mondays, she'd be flying out of bed every morning excited about the day to come because she was doing something she was passionate about. Instead of dropping her daughter off at a babysitter every day, she'd get to spend more time with her and experience the joy of her growing up. Janet would be living the life of her dreams.

Take some time out to think about the story of your own life. Are you doing the things that will allow you to live the life you really want? Or do you find yourself falling victim to inhibiting tactics and psychological roadblocks that prevent you from doing so? If you have answered yes to this question, keep reading because the following chapters will equip you with the tools required to help you live the life you know you truly deserve.

CHAPTER 3:

GET YOUR MIND RIGHT

Before you even start looking at ways to overcome procrastination, it's important to understand that beating it is 100% mental effort! There is no magic pill you can take or fail-proof strategy you can implement to push through. It takes a cognitive effort to keep going when you don't feel like it and when there are obstacles hindering your progress.

Your mindset determines the way you look at a situation. The right mindset is all it takes to find the motivation and the will required to follow through on something.

Donald wanted to start his own business. He loved the idea of one day becoming a self-sufficient entrepreneur who could give his family the best of everything. His idol was Steve Jobs; he wanted to be just as rich as he was, and while he knew that success didn't come easily, he wasn't aware of how difficult it would be.

When he embarked on the journey of starting his own business, he encountered a multitude of challenges that scared him. For example, he had to make a large financial investment, and he was afraid that if he took the risk and lost all his money, he wouldn't be able to survive. Donald was not very comfortable with this uncertainty. He also didn't like the fact that in order to make this work, he needed to budget and cut out certain luxuries that he enjoyed.

Instead of adapting to this temporary uncomfortable situation and embracing the things he was afraid of, Donald decided to abandon his dream. He enjoyed thinking about that lifestyle, but he wasn't prepared to make the sacrifices required to achieve it. As a result, Donald settled back into the job that he didn't like, just because he was comfortable with it. He remained 'an average Joe' and never accomplished his goals.

Donald had a negative mindset; he did not want to endure the discomfort associated with making sacrifices. He was not willing to step into the uncertainty of the unknown even though he knew he wasn't satisfied with his life. He focused on the negative aspects of achieving his dreams and was too afraid to see what was waiting for him on the other side of his fears.

Donald could have been successful if he'd adopted a different mindset, but he had an inflexible mentality that caused him to look at problems in the wrong way. If he had chosen to get comfortable with discomfort, he would have accepted that status as his temporary 'new normal' and persevered with the vision. Eventually, when he was living the life of his dreams, he would have looked back and realized that the sacrifice was worth it.

Mindset 1 - It's Worth it: Why do you want to achieve your goals? Most people don't set goals for the sake of it. They do so because something is driving them, which makes all the hard work required to achieve something more than worth it.

When you understand why you do something and how it contributes to your end goal, it will give you the motivation to continue. When you assign value to the things you do and remember that every action is taking you one step closer to where you want to go in life, you will quickly overcome procrastination. For example, when you feel that some of the classes you are taking for your degree are a waste of time, you tend to do your assignments at the last minute because you have zero interest in the subject. You can fix this mindset by remembering that the classes are not pointless; they are an important part of your degree, and by taking them, you are getting one step closer to your graduation so that you can land your dream job at the end of it.

Mindset 2 - Comfort and Discomfort: Another important aspect to understand on your journey to success is that discomfort will become your new normal. You will need to get comfortable with being uncomfortable. You will never feel comfortable doing the things that are required to achieve your goals because you are taking on new challenges that you have never encountered. For example, if you want the body of your dreams, you will need to get used to the feeling of sore muscles. If you are going to take a day off every time you are in pain, don't expect to get rid of those love handles!

There is nothing comfortable about change. If you are going to succeed at anything in life, this is something you will need to accept. To get used to change, try doing new things that are outside your comfort zone, including learning new skills, speaking to people you wouldn't normally talk to, and practicing things you know you are not good at until you get good at them. The more you expose yourself to situations and things that you are uncomfortable with, the more quickly you will get comfortable with discomfort.

Mindset 3 - Education: I am not talking about education in the traditional sense of the word. There is nothing wrong with going to college and earning a degree to gain access to your chosen field. However, it is important to understand that learning doesn't stop when you finish high school *or* college. Life should be about continuous improvement. Whatever you want to achieve, there are books you can read, seminars you can attend, and courses you can take. Get into the habit of knowledge seeking, because as the saying goes, the more you learn, the more you earn! Lifelong learners know this is true.

Now that you've got your mind right, it's time to learn how to crush procrastination for good!

CHAPTER 4:

THE SCIENCE BEHIND CRUSHING PROCRASTINATION

Sarah is about to start working on a large project. She knows that if she is going to meet her deadline, she will need to complete 20 pages of code per day. Every time she goes to start on the job, she doesn't feel like it and puts it off and promises herself she will do 40 pages the next day. The same thing happens the next day and it keeps on happening until the deadline is a couple of days away, and she's hardly written any code.

Sarah stays up all night. She submits the work on time, but it's full of mistakes. There were several problems with the code that she didn't have time to resolve because she had left the project until the last minute. The client is not happy with the work. Not only does he reject it, but he writes her a bad review and she doesn't get paid for the job.

Edna works on a similar project. Unlike Sarah, Edna recognizes that there are always problems with coding, and so she ensures she has enough time to iron out any issues when they arise. She splits her work into small, manageable chunks of 20 pages per day and rewards herself each time she completes a section. Even though Edna has given herself a target of 20 pages per day, she usually exceeds this and writes about 25 pages. At the end of the week, Edna has completed the job and sends it to her client who is very happy with it. Not only does he write her a glowing five-star review, he hires her again and recommends Edna to one of his friends.

Sarah and Edna are both coders. They are both equally intelligent, but Sarah is always rushing her work, which causes her to make careless mistakes. On the other hand, Edna not only submits error-free work, but it is always before the deadline. The difference between Edna and Sarah is that Edna uses a system called "temptation bundling" to ensure that she doesn't procrastinate. The system gives her plenty of time to find and fix bugs as well as write the code. Sarah doesn't have a system; she just makes herself promises and goes with the flow but ends up doing everything at the last minute. Can you see how procrastination leads to frustration, stress, and sloppy work?

Everyone knows what procrastination is, but why is it such a common problem for people?

Time Inconsistency: This is a self-sabotaging habit in which we value instant gratification over long-term rewards. Take a minute to think about the following scenario. Imagine that you have two selves: a present and a future self. The goals you set for yourself now are plans for your future self. Planning for your future self is an easy task. You can have a lot of fun envisioning what your life will be like in ten years' time. You will also find it enjoyable to do things like make a vision board and write out your list of goals.

However, your future self does not play a role in creating your future self, only your present self can do that by taking action. Unfortunately, your present self wants to enjoy the spoils of instant gratification. You don't have enough patience to wait to reap the rewards associated with the hard work required to develop your future self. Therefore, you do everything you can to avoid doing anything that you are not going to reap immediate benefits from. For example, you want a side income so you can pay off your mortgage within 5 years. You have managed to secure a few contracts outside of your day job, but instead of working on them, you take naps whenever you feel tired and then wake up a couple of hours later regretting that you had taken a nap! So everything your present self is doing is sabotaging any possibility of your future self being able to live the life it wants to live.

The most effective way to overcome time inconsistency is to develop a reward system that will benefit you now, but won't hinder the manifestation of your future self. Waiting for future rewards is often not enough to motivate your present self, because your present self wants instant gratification. One of the most effective ways to overcome this hurdle is through temptation bundling.

Temptation Bundling: Temptation bundling is a powerful way to eliminate procrastination and boost productivity because it combines your present and future self and your conflicting needs. Behavioral expert Katy Milkman from the University of Pennsylvania developed the concept. It involves allowing yourself to indulge in instant gratification at the same time as achieving the goals required to benefit your future self. It sounds complicated, but trust me, it's not!

Basically, you create and establish a good habit you are struggling with that will benefit you in the long term and feel good now as well. Think about working out at the same time you are watching your favorite TV show or soaking your feet in warm salt water while you are working on your book. Can you see how you are reaping the benefit of instant gratification at the same time as doing the things required to achieve your goals?

One of the main reasons people find it difficult to stay motivated is that hard work isn't pleasant. But you can avoid the suffering associated with hard work by bundling your temptations in with your long-term goals.

Milkman discovered that approximately 51% of participants in her study were willing to exercise with temptation bundling.

How to Apply Temptation Bundling: Get a pen and paper and draw a line down the middle of the paper. On one side, make a list of your guilty pleasures and temptations, and on the other side, the things you need to do to achieve your goals. Then come up with some creative ways to connect them.

Let's say you enjoy running, soccer, and surfing, but piano lessons, homework, and work commitments stand in your way. How can you combine these things to make the things you don't enjoy more tolerable? Use the reward system to encourage you to finish the important tasks first. For example, you might give yourself the challenge of completing a one-hour piano lesson before going out to play soccer. There are also several other psychological tricks you can use to get moving in the right direction.

Start Small: One way to prevent procrastination is to start small. Break your tasks down into the smallest possible components and that will make your first step extremely easy. When it comes to working on the things we don't enjoy, taking the first step is the hardest part. However, when that step is a small one, it becomes a lot easier to take.

You can compare procrastination to a giant wall you've got to climb. If you collect enough small rocks and pebbles, you will eventually create a step for yourself that is high enough for you to get over the wall without further effort. You could also spend your time looking for large boulders to help you get over the wall, but you will need much more effort to collect them, and the thought of the effort required will be off-putting enough that you never even start.

The idea is to make sure that you set yourself a very low barrier to get started. For example, if you have set yourself a goal of losing 100 pounds, you can start your weight loss journey by taking a ten-minute walk every morning.

There are two key parts to starting small; the first is to break your task down into small manageable steps. Using the weight loss example—instead of looking at the 100 pounds you need to lose, set a goal of losing 1 pound per week by going on 10-minute walks and eating fewer carbohydrates and more vegetables instead. In this way, you eliminate inertia and build forward momentum.

The second part involves starting with the easiest task first, which might seem slightly counterintuitive. After all, why would you leave the more difficult tasks until the end? Don't you want to get them out of the way first? Remember, beating procrastination is about getting started, and the easier the first step is, the likelier you are to get started. You are proving to your mind and encouraging yourself that it is possible to complete the task by starting small, and by the time you get to the more difficult part of the task, you will be mentally prepared to take on the rest.

Inertia is resistance to change. The more you lounge on the couch watching Netflix, the less likely you are to start working on the important things. The opposite of inertia is momentum, which provides you with the drive required to keep moving forward. Your aim is to eliminate inertia and build momentum, and the easiest way to do this is to start small.

Let's say you are writing your final year dissertation for your postgraduate degree. It's fifteen thousand words long and the thought of it is so daunting it's making you depressed. How do you get over this hurdle? As I have mentioned, you should start by breaking the dissertation down into small manageable chunks. If you aim to write 200 words a day five days a week, you will complete the project within 15 weeks if you stick to your schedule.

The easiest parts of the dissertation will be research and the outline, so get on with these parts first because they will take the least amount of effort. Once you have completed the easy parts, you will have built up enough momentum to start working on the more difficult parts of the project, and you won't feel that overwhelming sense of frustration that causes you to keep putting things off.

THINK ABOUT WHAT COULD GO WRONG

Another strategy to consider is thinking about the things that could go wrong with the task you are working on. Highly productive and successful people such as Bill Gates are hyper vigilant when evaluating what could go wrong. In his book *Great by Choice*, Jim Collins discusses this tactic in depth. He refers to it as "productive paranoia." He talks about people like Bill Gates who are always paranoid about the things that might go wrong.

By always doing what they can to avoid the worst and planning for the worst, it leads these people to work excessively hard. They focus on their projects at all times to ensure that the worst possible scenarios don't become a reality. Fear motivates them and eliminates procrastination.

Use productive paranoia to evaluate what could go wrong with your project. Develop contingency plans to work around the problems if they do occur. Like Bill Gates and other highly successful people, it will cause you to become more productive and efficient in everything that you do.

You should also think about the consequences of not taking action. For example, if you are looking for a new job and you come across one you are interested in, but instead of applying for the position immediately, you decide to watch your favorite TV show instead. A consequence could be that the job post might get taken down before you've finished watching your program because it has enough applicants already. Because of procrastination, you missed an opportunity to apply for a job that could have changed your life. The fear of losing out can be an effective motivator; fear is not a pleasant motivator, but it's effective, and if it works, use it!

There are several underlying reasons for procrastination, including safety, complacency, and boredom. Once these feelings have been stripped away, you are left determined to avoid negative consequences. As mentioned, there is nothing fun about using fear as a motivator, so only use it in small doses and as a last resort.

Some really interesting factors contribute to procrastination and a lack of productivity—turn to the next chapter to find out what they are.

CHAPTER 5:

EAT TO WIN

When we consider the factors that contribute to our productivity, we rarely think about food. For those of us who are struggling to stay on top of deadlines, meetings, and emails, food is nothing but the fuel that gives us the energy to keep going for a couple more hours.

The food that we eat has more of an effect on us than we realize. When you fill up your car, you can expect it to run regardless of the brand of gas you put in it. The same doesn't apply with food. Think about this for a minute, if filling your tank up at Shell meant that you could avoid all traffic and arrive at your destination in record time, but filling up at Exxon meant that you were unable to drive more than 10 miles per hour, which gas station would you use to fill up your car? This sounds like a trick question, but it isn't. I am guessing that each one of you would choose to fill up at Shell, right?

Food and our cognitive performance are directly related, which is why making the wrong food choices can have such a negative effect on your day. Every function in the body needs energy to do its job, and that includes the digestive system. Your body doesn't have an unlimited supply of energy, which is why it's so important to pay special attention to your dietary habits.

Eating the wrong foods can seriously impair your productivity. Think about what happens when you've just eaten a large plate of spaghetti? All you want to do is lie down. You know you've got work to do but the food you've eaten has completely sapped your energy. You assume you are just tired, but there is more to it than that.

Watch Your Carbs

Nobody is arguing against the fact that carbohydrates are a necessary part of a healthy diet, but it's the type and quantity of carbs we consume that matters. Carbs are generally found in bread and sugary foods. High carbohydrate foods cause the body to produce excess amounts of insulin, which then causes the body to produce high levels of sleep hormones such as tryptophan and serotonin. What happens when you feel sleepy? You can't concentrate because all you want to do is take a nap, and this causes your productivity levels to plummet.

Low Blood Sugar = No Will Power

Self-control and productivity go hand in hand. The majority of the important things that we need to do are far from exciting. If you are writing a book and you set a goal of writing 1,000 words per day, unless you are extremely disciplined, you are going to find every excuse not to do it. The same goes for exercising and working on anything that's going to enhance the quality of your life. It's human nature to want to take the easy way out.

Here is a list of some of the most effective brainpower boosting foods:

Chickpeas: Chickpeas are high in magnesium, an important dietary source. Magnesium plays an essential role in energy metabolism and speeding up messaging to the brain. Magnesium also causes the blood vessels to relax, which increases the amount of blood that flows to the brain. Studies show that the majority of Western diets are low in magnesium and that most adults on average consume only 66 percent of the recommended daily allowance of magnesium. Research has also found that stress drains the body's supply of magnesium.

Magnesium is not the most popular mineral, and it's typically found in foods that most people have never heard of. For example, kelp is a potent source of magnesium with 780 mg per serving, but how many people have kelp on their shopping list? The alternative is chickpeas, one serving, which is one cup, contains 220 mg of magnesium, or hummus, which is made from chickpeas.

Crab: You rarely see crab on power food lists. Why is beyond my comprehension, but it should be right up there with the best of them in my opinion. One serving of crab contains 1840 mg of the amino acid phenylalanine. It is needed so that the body can produce dopamine, noradrenaline, adrenaline, and the thyroid hormone. A lot of seafood and fish are high in phenylalanine, but I've chosen crab because it's less likely to have a high mercury content and is easier to find.

Research has found that phenylalanine also may play a role in combating Parkinson's disease. Just for the record, crab is a great dietary source for vitamin B12, with one serving containing 192 percent of your daily requirement.

Walnuts: Walnuts are high in omega-3 fatty acids, and research suggests that omega-3 fatty acids boost the function of neurotransmitters in the brain. One study discovered that elderly people who had high levels of omega-3 fatty acids in their blood, especially docosahexaenoic acid (DHA), had a larger brain volume and got higher test results for cognitive and memory. Omega-3s are also good for the heart. They prevent the arteries from getting clogged up, which speeds up blood circulation, benefitting the brain.

Although salmon is the most popular source of omega-3, it is high in mercury. You can eat as many walnuts as you like without worrying about any adverse side effects. You can sprinkle them over a salad or eat them as a snack in between meals. Walnuts also contain vitamin B6, which is good for memory.

Buckwheat: Buckwheat is a natural mood enhancer; it calms emotions and causes the body to relax. Buckwheat is high in tryptophan, one serving, which is one cup, provides 25 percent of your recommended daily allowance. Buckwheat also contains 229mg per serving of magnesium. This superfood is a fruit seed that's high in fiber and gluten free, making it a great grain substitute. You can cook it and add it to a salad, or you can add it to a stew. You can also boil it for breakfast, similar to cream of wheat or grits.

Celery: In 2010, researchers discovered that the plant compound luteolin reduces the rates of age-related memory loss and inflammation in the brain, which experts now believe is the main cause of neurodegeneration. By blocking the action of inflammatory cytokines, it appears that luteolin prevents the cycle of degenerative changes in the brain. Celery contains the highest amount of luteolin, and other good sources include carrots and peppers.

Turmeric: The spice that gives mustard and curry their yellow color contains curcumin. Researchers have discovered that it can stimulate neurogenesis, which is the process of creating new brain cells. It also slows down the progression of Alzheimer's and boosts memory.

Red Meat: There are many reasons not to eat too much red meat; however, in moderation, it has major benefits. Red meat is high in vitamin B12, which boosts energy and is essential for healthy brain function. B12 is so important that a deficiency causes brain and nerve damage. If you want a good source of B12, you might want to add some beef liver to your diet.

Blueberries: You've probably heard all about the many health benefits of blueberries, but let me remind you once again. Research has found that blueberries are linked to improved memory retention, sharper thinking, and faster learning.

Start adding these foods to your diet and watch your productivity soar! A healthy diet and exercise go hand in hand. Let's take a look at how getting the blood flowing around your body can help you fight the procrastination trap!

CHAPTER 6:

RUN TOWARD YOUR VISION

Statistics show that the majority of people don't exercise. There are many reasons for this, but one of them is procrastination. Just think about how many times you've said you'd start going to the gym or start jogging but kept putting it off until tomorrow? Exercise is an important ingredient when it comes to overcoming procrastination. You will find it's a habit that most successful people have adopted.

Starbucks President Michelle Gass is out running by 4:30 am every morning. Vogue editor Anna Wintour is slamming tennis balls by 6:00 a.m., and founder of the Virgin Group Richard Branson starts his day with a run. These are some of the most successful people in the world, and they clearly know something that the average Joe doesn't if they are all doing some version of it! There is more to exercising than fitting into your skinny jeans or showing off your six-pack in a tank top. Exercise is not only good for your health, but it supercharges your productivity. Here are some reasons why:

EXERCISE KEEPS YOU FOCUSED AND ALERT

If you hated science at school, I apologize in advance. Exercise stimulates the flow of blood causing it to travel to the brain at an accelerated pace. When there is more blood flowing around your cranium, it increases your awareness and sharpness. University of Bristol professor Jim McKenna conducted a study and found that exercise improved work performance, mental sharpness, and time management.

EXERCISE INCREASES YOUR ENERGY LEVELS

There are going to be days when you simply can't be bothered to exercise before or after work. This makes absolutely no sense, but studies have found that it works. If you exercise when you don't have the energy, it will increase your energy levels. Energy improves your body's ability to transfer oxygen and glucose throughout the body and brain.

Researchers at The University of Georgia conducted a six-week study in which participants were split into three groups. Two groups did low to moderate intensity exercises and one group did no exercise. The two groups that exercised reported that they experienced an increase in their energy levels in comparison to the control group who did not exercise.

The bottom line is if you want to get anything done throughout the day, you need energy to do so. The more energy you have, the more you get done, so get moving!

EXERCISE ENHANCES BRAIN FUNCTION

Your 36 DDs or your Hulk Hogan style biceps are not your best asset, your brain is! To go to work every day and make money you need a fully functioning brain. Therefore, it makes sense to keep it sharp. According to the author of *Brain Rules* by John Medina, people who live a sedentary lifestyle score lower on cognitive tests than people who exercise. In a clinical trial conducted by Swinburne's University and The Brain Sciences Institute, there was an obvious link between brain function, physical fitness, and lower levels of work-related stress.

Lead researcher Paul Taylor stated that there was a definite improvement in the employee's cognition and mood. The exercise group showed a four percent increase in overall brain function. You are capable of making better decisions, concentrating, and focusing when your brain is functioning at full capacity. If you are going to be more efficient and effective, your brain must be working at its full potential.

Exercise Can Improve Creativity

Do you suffer from writer's block? Do you get stuck on a problem and spend hours trying to figure it out? If you have answered "yes" to either of these questions, you can break through the block by doing some exercise. *The Journal of Experimental Psychology* published a study that discovered that taking a walk, whether indoors or outdoors, fueled creative thinking. There was a 60 percent increase in creative output after a person went for a walk.

Exercise Improves Your Work-Life Balance

Adding exercise to your daily routine is not simply another activity to cross off your to-do list. The Harvard Business Review published an article stating that people who were committed to a daily workout found it easier to find a good work-life balance. This may be because structured activity helped to improve time management making them more confident in their ability to balance the demands of work and personal life.

Now that you understand the science behind beating procrastination, the importance of having the right mindset and the right foods to fuel your body for optimal performance, and you appreciate how exercise can get you moving in the right direction, the next step is to learn how to establish your goals effectively so that you have a tangible blueprint to follow.

CHAPTER 7:

WRITE DOWN THE VISION AND MAKE IT A PLAN

According to *Business Insider*, 80% of New Year's resolutions are abandoned by the second week in February. Outside of a lack of motivation, one of the main reasons is a failure to plan. This is not just about New Year's resolutions, it applies to goal setting in general. What people fail to understand is that there is a strategy involved with goal setting. Goals are typically verbalized; you will hear things such as "This year I plan to…"

- "Lose weight and get into shape"
- "Save more money"
- "Manage my time better"
- "Make new friends"

I could go on, but I think you get the point. These goals are great, but how are you going to go about fulfilling them? Here are some steps to assist you in getting from point A to point B:

The Importance of Setting Goals

Success is not an accident that the lucky few just happen to stumble upon. It is a decision that people make and they then do what is required of them to make sure that their dreams turn into reality. When you set goals for yourself, they provide you with a long-term vision and motivation to achieve short term goals.

By setting concise and well-defined goals, you enable yourself to keep track of them and feel a sense of satisfaction when you have accomplished them. When you articulate your dream on paper, a slow, long, and pointless uphill struggle turns into forward progress. As you begin to realize that you actually have the drive and the ability to achieve your goals, that will give you the confidence you need to keep pushing and overcome procrastination.

The Starting Line

Sit down with a notepad and pen and write your goals down onto paper. Thinking about your dream is never going to be enough. You need something tangible to look at that is going to motivate and inspire you to get on with it. You give your dreams creative reality when you can see them. Here is the process.

Start backward. It sounds weird, I know, but hear me out. Before you can achieve anything, you should be able to see it first. No, you are not crazy. When you can see things in your mind's eye that no one else can see, don't run away from it. That multibillion-dollar corporation that you are dreaming about is more real than you think.

The word "dream" has been grossly misused. The assumption is that because it can't be seen in the physical world, it can't be a reality. Some people get discouraged from achieving their goals when they tell someone about it, and the reply is, "Oh stop dreaming!" You might be working as a shop assistant without the relevant qualifications, so to everyone else your goals look impossible. Please remember that this is your dream and only you can turn it into a reality, regardless of the circumstances that you find yourself in at present.

If you are not too sure about the type of goals you need to set for yourself, here are some ideas to get your creative juices flowing:

- **Career Goals:** Where do you hope to be in your career in the next five years? A partner, a C.E.O., a manager?
- **Financial Goals:** Do you want to become a millionaire by a certain age? How do you intend to achieve this?
- **Education Goals:** Your career goals might mean that you are going to have to get certain qualifications to achieve them. You may need to go and get a degree in a certain subject, or get a real estate license.
- **Family Goals:** Do you want to get married and have children? How do you intend to become the best part-ner to your spouse? What kind of spouse are you look-ing for?
- **Physical Goals:** How much weight do you need to lose? Do you need to tone up? How do you intend to do this?

Spend some time brainstorming ideas and come up with a list of no more than 10 goals that you can focus on.

GOAL SETTING TIPS

- Turn all goals into positive present statements: For example, if you want to write a book within a year, write "I have written a book by the end of the year." When your goals are written in the present tense your subconscious mind is fooled into believing that it has already happened.

- Be Specific: If you don't know exactly what you want, you will never achieve it. Include details such as dates, amounts, and times because this will help you to measure your achievements.

Now that you have put your goals down on paper, they might look even scarier to you than when they were in your head! Not to worry, once you understand what it takes to stay in the game, you will have the ability to power through your goals like a pro!

CHAPTER 8:

DEVELOP STAYING POWER

Adele is an idealist, and so she established a charity to help underprivileged people. What she hadn't thought about were the many obstacles she would face as she embarked on her project. She was unaware that working for a non-profit organization still counted as a business and would involve a lot more than lending a helping hand to those who needed it.

Whenever she experienced challenges such as securing funding, marketing to generate interest in her cause, and dealing with competition from other organizations, she felt overwhelmed. Adele would think to herself, *"Why is it so difficult to get people to care about the needy the way I do?"*

After a while, Adele lost her passion and drive because she couldn't deal with the amount of negative feelings that came with it. She didn't like attending charity events or writing grant applications; and within a few months, she had given up on something she really cared about. Her friends and family members wanted to know why she had abandoned a cause that appeared to be so dear to her heart.

One of the main reasons for Adele's failure was her idealist nature, and while it's important to have an optimistic mindset, it's equally as important to understand that perfection doesn't exist, and you are always going to encounter obstacles. If she had anticipated and planned for any problems that could arise, she would have been prepared on some level to deal with them. Adele assumed that the majority of her time would be spent helping people and not doing things like securing funding and attending charity events.

Adele did not have a true source of motivation. If someone had asked her why she started the charity, her reason was not enough to carry her through the trials she faced while pursuing her goal. Thinking about why she started would have kept her eyes focused on the prize, but the reality is that she didn't know why she started in the first place. Neither was she able to comprehend that every hindrance was a part of the process and that ultimately it would lead to the fulfillment of her dream.

Sometimes, we don't follow through because we simply don't have the passion for what we are doing, and we lose motivation because we have no interest in it. That makes sense; but caring about something is not always enough to see it through to the end, there are times when we just don't have the drive to get things done.

A lack of drive is caused by the inability to connect with three main aspects. These are: first, what the things we care about represent; second, the benefits associated with our positive actions; and third, the negative consequences associated with our failure to follow through. These three aspects combined create motivation.

Motivation comes from the things that drive you to work toward your goals and encourage you to persevere in the face of adversity. Motivation is defined through the framework of external and internal motivators.

External Motivators: These are the factors outside of yourself that motivate you to take action. They are circumstances or people that drive you. External motivators also are connected to avoiding negative consequences. For example, you could be determined not to fail to avoid disappointing your family. Your fear of losing your job might drive you to work harder than normal. If you allow them to work for you, external motivators are extremely beneficial because your desire to avoid the negative consequences associated with inaction will push you in the right direction. We all want to avoid suffering. If you know that failing to follow through will lead to some sort of pain, you are going to do what is necessary to avoid those consequences.

Accountability Partners: These are people who hold you accountable for your actions. Your accountability partner will remind you of the things you need to get done, they will chastise you when you don't do the things you said you were going to do. They will encourage you when you want to give up. It's because you don't want to disappoint this person or feel as if you are wasting their time, that you are going to get things done.

Accountability Group: Holding yourself accountable to a group of people can be more effective than being accountable to a single person. For one, the disappointment and shame is intensified when multiple people are involved; and two, you will always have someone that you are accountable to if one person decides to pull out or they become unavailable.

Financial Investment: Investing money into a project will always keep your attention on it. We value what we pay for.

For example, you may pay to take a course or buy expensive equipment, and then you make sure you finish what you started because you don't want your money to be wasted. The main motivator here is to avoid spending money on something and never getting the benefit out of it.

If you've got the resources, you can take the financial investment motivator to the next level by hiring someone, such as a coach or a personal trainer, to help you. When you are paying someone to hold you accountable, not only will you have wasted your money if you don't follow through, but the person you hire wants to do their job properly, so they are not going to allow you to slack.

Self-Bribery: This involves bribing yourself with a reward if you follow through. You allow the reward to push you to achieve your goals. For example, you might want to go on a cruise with friends, and you know that if you save money wisely, you can afford to go. The thought of the vacation will motivate you to put away your wallet any time you are tempted to buy something you don't need.

External motivators are typically about avoiding negative consequences; therefore, think about the things you want to avoid; and if you can't think of anything, create them. Once you have decided on the negative consequences you don't want to experience, allow them to drive you to work toward your goals.

Internal Motivators: Internal motivators are related to the things you want as opposed to avoiding punishment or negative consequences. The problem with negative consequences is that despite how much you don't want to experience them, at some point, you will realize that they won't kill you—and as a result, your motivation goes out the window because you can just learn to deal with the consequences.

Sometimes, fear and external motivators are not enough to push you, but the things you want, and love are. However, this all depends on what you are driven by. If you are motivated by the fear of negative consequences, then external motivation will work well for you. But internal motivation is ideal when you are deeply passionate about what you want.

Internal motivators are connected to the reasons why you are working toward a specific goal. The more reasons you have, the more likely you are to finish what you started. Ask yourself the following questions to determine the benefits you will gain from following through and allow those desires to drive you:

- *What will you gain from this?* Is it happiness or fulfillment?
- *How will it change your life?* Will you be able to buy your dream home? Buy your dream car? Move to another country? Or care for a sick relative?
- *How will your family benefit?* Does your family mean a lot to you? What will it mean to your family if you succeed in your endeavor? Think about the joy on their faces and the life you can give your children. You will be able to move to a better neighborhood or afford to send them to private school or college.
- *How will it impact others?* Does the well-being of others depend on your success? Will you become a role model to youth? Will you be able to inspire and motivate other people to turn their dreams into a reality? Will it mean you can make a substantial donation to a charity of your choice?
- *How will it make you feel?* Think about the high levels of self-esteem, pride, and happiness you will feel if you accomplish your goals.

Internal motivators are powerful motivating forces that will drive you to maximize your potential. They are the things that will push you when the road gets rocky and you are considering throwing in the towel. Finishing what you start becomes a lot easier when you are focused on how your world will benefit. So whenever you need to do something you don't enjoy, or when you start getting tired or bored, think about these motivators when working on your goals. Think about how what you are doing will bring you one step closer to turning your dreams into a reality. Think about how awesome you will feel when you finish. Spend some time each day reviewing your goals and reminding yourself of why you want to complete them. Allow those reasons to fill you with the motivation required to drive you to complete your project.

Write down the answers to these questions; and every so often, review them to remind yourself of why you need to achieve your goals.

THE POWER OF OPPORTUNITY COST

You will never escape the sacrifice associated with finishing what you start. You will need to spend time, money, and effort to commit to accomplishing your goals. It is human nature not to like sacrifices. For example, if you could lie in bed until midday and eat junk food for every meal *and* still remain healthy and get the body of your dreams, you are not going to wake up at 5 a.m. to go to the gym, are you? Therefore, what motivates you must be powerful enough to make the sacrifice worthwhile.

There is an opportunity cost associated with everything we do in life; this means that we must give something up to get something back. If you want to become an expert at playing the piano, you will need to sacrifice the time you spend on other leisure activities to perfect your skill. If you want to earn a degree, not only will you need to spend time traveling to and from college, you will need to wake up a little bit earlier, and maybe go to bed slightly later to accommodate studying. The question is: "Are you willing to make the trade-off?"

The term is called "opportunity cost" because if you are not willing to pay the price (giving up something) for the chance to get what you want, you are not going to follow through. Therefore, you need a motivator that drives you to believe the opportunity cost is worth it. You can resolve this issue in two ways. First, your motivation must be stronger than the opportunity cost, and second, you can make your sacrifices smaller. In other words, you minimize the pain associated with taking action. In both cases, the cost-benefit analysis must have more benefits attached to it.

For example, your sacrifice might involve going to an evening accounting class instead of going out with friends on a Friday night. You need to pass this class to get onto the degree track required to get your dream job, but you really enjoy meeting up with your friends on a Friday night. However, you should think about how much better your life would be by sacrificing a few Friday nights out. If not, you will find the conflict too difficult, and forfeit your dream job for something that you will probably grow out of in a few years anyway.

Let's see how this works out with the second solution. Instead of sacrificing your Friday nights, you might want to try arranging to go out on another night; or, if possible, don't spend as *much* time with your friends and meet up with them after class. In this way, you are still making a sacrifice, but it isn't as big—does that make sense to you? With this option, you can still go out with your friends and work on your goals at the same time.

When confronted with opportunity cost and sacrifice, re-member that you will need to make some changes; there is no way around this. But if you focus on minimizing the sacrifice and increasing the benefit, you will feel a lot more motivated when working toward your goals.

KEEP YOUR MIND ON YOUR MOTIVATION

Internal and external motivators really help to boost the com-mitment and productivity needed to follow through. But if you keep forgetting about them, they won't help much. According to the American Psychological Association, working on your goals is more likely if you are exposed to the stimuli that motivate you. Hearing or seeing your motivators will drive you to keep going. We think about so many things throughout the day that it's easy to get lost in a sea of fruitless thoughts that have nothing to do with our end goal. Katherine Milkman from the Univer-sity of Pennsylvania endorsed this idea. She states that reminders through association assist people in remembering goals and tak-ing action to accomplish them.

Milkman came to this conclusion after conducting a study with a group of participants who were asked to take part in an hour-long computer assignment. If they completed it, a dol-lar would be donated to the local food bank and they would also get compensation. Once they received their compensation, they were asked to make their donations by picking up paper-clips. The control group was given these instructions and then thanked for their time. The test group was told that they could find the paper clips next to an elephant statue.

At the end of the study, the results showed that 74% of the participants who were told that the paperclips were near the elephant statue remembered to collect them. But only 42% of the other group remembered to collect the paper clips. The participants found it easier to remember the paper clips because the elephant statue acted as a visual cue for them. When the participants saw the odd-looking statue, they were reminded of what they were instructed to do.

Additionally, Milkman and Rogers found that very obvious cues were more effective than cues that didn't stand out as much. For example, a visual cue like one of the aliens from *Toy Story* was a better reminder than a written one. Therefore, if you want to increase your chances of success, expose yourself to your motivators continuously.

However, it is also important that these cues stand out and are impossible to ignore. You can also incorporate other sensory inputs such as scents, textures, and sounds. Put a picture of your child on your desk to remind yourself that you need to secure your financial future to give them a better life.

You can put the picture in a frame that smells like your child's bubble bath, or if it's your partner, like their cologne or perfume. To clarify, I am not just talking about sticking post-it notes all over the house, you should get really imaginative and creative. It is also important to move the cues around every few days so that you don't get too comfortable with them and start seeing them as a part of the furniture.

Finally, another way to keep things fresh in your mind and to keep you motivated is to write your motivators out every few days, but use different wording.

The government has a manifesto. You probably have a manifesto or mission statement at work, so why not consider creating your own manifesto to help you overcome procrastination? Find out how to do this in the next chapter.

CHAPTER 9:

CREATE A PERSONAL MANIFESTO

As I have mentioned throughout this book, there are going to be bumps in the road when you set out on your journey to achieve your goals, and it will be during these times that you will feel a strong urge to give up. Instead of digging deep into your willpower reserves, developing a set of rules for yourself will help you make important decisions when you get to that fork in the road.

Since childhood, we have been told that we must follow the rules. Well, this time, you get to make your own rules that will help you get exactly what you want. We will refer to these rules as "mental models," and they are essential when it comes to following through because they provide you with a specific method for decision-making. By the way, there are no exceptions to this rule. They will ensure that you stop making the wrong decisions based on a lack of self-discipline and willpower.

Rules hold you accountable. They ensure that you don't wander through your days with no direction. Your rules will make your decisions for you. An example of a rule is that you must complete, in a specific time frame, two tasks on your to-do list that are related to your end goal. If you stick to this rule, even when you don't feel like it, you will eventually accomplish what you set out to do.

David is a writer, and in the morning, he gets really excited when he tells himself that he will start writing his novel after work. As the day goes on, he starts getting tired, and the inspiration he had in the morning has disappeared. All he wants to do when he gets home from work is sit in front of the TV and eat pizza. Because he hasn't established a rule, he never makes any progress. He feels distressed about his inability to get started, and before David goes to bed, he makes a promise to himself that he will write two chapters the next day to make up for it.

Guess what? A week has come and gone, and David still hasn't gotten started on his novel! He uses the excuse that his day job is too demanding, and he feels too drained and tired when he gets home to start writing. Additionally, since he keeps making promises to himself by adding more chapters to his goal, he feels even more intimidated at the prospect of getting started. If he didn't have the energy to write one chapter a week ago, he definitely won't have the energy to write four chapters now. As a result, he feels too overwhelmed and never gets started because he always has an excuse not to. David gave himself too much leeway, which ultimately led to self-sabotage.

Now, let's suppose David applied a strict rule that doesn't tolerate any excuses. No matter how uninspired and tired he feels, he knows he's got to write one chapter of his book every night. When he gets home from work, he looks at his laptop but would rather sit in front of the TV instead.

However, he is reminded of his rule and decides to get a cup of coffee and get on with it. He goes to bed at the end of the night totally exhausted, but proud of himself and content. He has finally started making progress with his book, and within a few months, he has completed it. David looks back and realizes that his accomplishment was more than worth the exhaustion every night after completing a chapter of his book.

Rules put a limit on your vision—they help you focus on the things that are most important to you. They stop you from spending hours on social media or clicking through YouTube videos when you know you've got a job to do. Here are some rules you can apply to your manifesto—feel free to add more if you wish.

Rule 1: Assess Yourself

Ask yourself why you make the decisions that you do. If it weren't out of fear or laziness, would you still give up? Answering this question makes you aware that you are not acting out of a lack of talent or ability, but your problem is that you are not willing to put in the hard work required to accomplish your goals. When you can accept that fear or laziness is the reason for your stagnation, it will encourage you to abandon these negative traits—this reality will drive you to take action.

When you face the fact that the only thing standing in your way is laziness or fear, you will quickly stop procrastinating and get on with it. So, before you kick your shoes off and decide to lie on the couch scrolling through Instagram, ask yourself whether it's fear or laziness that is preventing you from taking action. When you start doing the best that you can do instead of the bare minimum, you will feel better about yourself.

Rule 2: A Maximum of Three Tasks

Sometimes we overwhelm ourselves by putting too many things on our to-do lists. The biggest de-motivator is to pick up your notepad and see 20 items staring back at you! The cure for this is usually to drop the notepad and go off and do something that isn't going to take so much energy, like watch TV!

By applying the 'three tasks maximum' rule, you avoid the problem of becoming overwhelmed because you only have to focus on three things. The night before, think about the three most important tasks you need to complete, then write them down in order of importance and decide what steps you will need to take to complete these tasks.

Once you get working on your tasks, you will also need to differentiate between actual action and pointless motion. Sometimes we can get so caught up in the preparation stage that we never get anything done. For example, if your goal is to read three chapters of a book that will help you establish your business, you might spend all your time arranging your desk convincing yourself that you are preparing to read. But because of all the energy you've spent on arranging the desk that really didn't need arranging in the first place, you end up reading one chapter instead of three. This is a dangerous form of procrastination because you believe you are moving forward, when in reality, you are going backward.

Rule 3: Create a Code of Conduct

Create a strict code of conduct that will force you to become more disciplined and follow through with your tasks. Write your code out in detail and position it somewhere that you will see it every day. Each item on your code of conduct may not apply to you daily, but it will help push you in the right direction when you start going off track. The rules should focus on creating requirements or limitations for your daily tasks so that you actually take action and get things done.

A code of conduct will force you to determine what you really want and need and evaluate what you hope to achieve. Basically, you are checking in on yourself to see how much progress you have made toward your end goal. It increases your focus on your intentions and helps you clarify them, so they become an important part of your work ethic. As a result, when you set out to achieve something, you have a rule in place that will encourage you to follow through on the project.

Give yourself five daily requirements and five daily limitations. Make clear statements to determine what you can and cannot do.

When it comes to requirements, remember that you are not a superhuman, so don't give yourself too much to do. Instead, find a way of working smarter, not harder, and give yourself five requirements that you know you will be able to meet realistically. Your requirements might involve reading one chapter of a book per day or completing a minimum of three hours of work before taking a lunch break.

Limitations restrict giving in to temptation and distraction, so choose the five things that tempt and distract you the most and put a limit on them. For example, if TV is your weakness, set a limit that you can only watch one hour of TV per day. Or you can only take an hour's lunch break, or you can only reply to social media messages for one hour a day.

RULE 4: REVISIT YOUR INTENSIONS

Rule 4 is like the first rule. You are going to have days when you simply can't be bothered, and you would rather have an early-to-bed night than work on your goals. When you revisit your intentions, you are reminding yourself what you want to achieve and why it's important that you get to work instead of pulling the duvet over your head. Get a pen and paper and write down the following three statements:

1. *"I want…"* Write out your end goal, how you are going to benefit from it, and your motivation for wanting to achieve it. Remind yourself of the internal or external motivators that are driving you. You might write something like, "I want to become a New York Times best-selling author," or, "I want to own my own business in the next two years."

2. *"I will…"* Write out how you intend to accomplish your goal and all the work you need to do to get there. This statement will remind you that the journey is just as important as the end goal; because without it, you will never reach your final destination. You might write something like, "I will read one book a week on how to start a business," or, "I will send out 100 extra cold emails per week to generate more clients."

3. *"I won't…"* Write out everything that you will not do to sabotage your chances of accomplishing your goals. You might write something like, "I won't spend 2 hours a night speaking to James," or, "I won't watch a movie instead of completing my tasks."

Any time you face a challenge and feel like giving up, read these statements and remind yourself of the reasons you have to push through no matter how hard things get. You will have noticed that the running theme throughout this book is repetition; because the more you remind yourself of why you do things like wake up at 4 am, why you no longer go out on Friday nights, or why you are so strict with your budget, the more likely you are to follow through with your goals.

RULE 5: THE 10-10-10 RULE

The next time you think about giving in to temptation, take a step back and think about how you will feel 10 minutes, 10 hours, or 10 days from now. This rule is very effective because it forces you to think about the person you would like to become in the future and how the decisions you make now will have a positive or negative effect on that person. We always know that when we give in to temptation, it is never good for us, but seldom do we consider specifically how it will affect us in the future.

Think about it like this: one soda isn't going to give you diabetes today, but if you give in now, you are going to give in again and again and again. Each time you indulge in your bad habit you will tell yourself that you will start "being good" again tomorrow, and tomorrow never comes. Five years down the line you are at the doctor's office being told you have diabetes and you will need to take insulin for the rest of your life. In that moment, you remember how many times you said you'd start eating healthy tomorrow, and now it's too late.

The decisions you make today are either going to take you one step closer toward accomplishing your goals or take you further away from them. When you apply the 10-10-10 rule and you feel a sense of guilt and regret, you know you are heading down the wrong path and it's time to turn back.

Starting is the most important part of overcoming procrastination. Once you take one step, you can take the next more easily. But some people fail to get started because they are dealing with too much junk. You can overcome this by following the steps set out in the next chapter.

CHAPTER 10:

HOW TO DECLUTTER YOUR MIND TO BEAT PROCRASTINATION

Momentum is a term often used in sports to describe an unstoppable team. But it originates from physics and refers to the quality of motion that an object has. Likewise, when you are striving toward your goals, you have momentum. It means that you are no longer sitting and staring at your vision board, but you are doing what is required to achieve your goals. However, getting started is what people struggle with the most, so here are some tips to get you moving in the right direction:

DECLUTTER

Do you feel stuck and overwhelmed and wish you could have enough peace so that you can think straight? One of the reasons you feel this way is because your mind is filled with clutter.

Instead of having the laser-sharp focus required to achieve your goals, your mind is scattered in all directions and all over the place. Think about it like this: it takes a magnifying glass being placed in the right position before the sun can pierce through it and set the piece of paper behind the magnifying glass on fire. When it's in the wrong position, the sunlight is fragmented, which diminishes its power. The same is true with your mind, when you don't have a clear purpose, non-essentials take over and you end up trying to do too many things at once, which leaves you exhausted and stressed at the end of the day. If you are going to move toward your goals freely and effortlessly, the first step is to *declutter.*

The Things You Can't Control: Worry is one of the main reasons for procrastination. We spend countless hours worrying about present events, past events, and future events. Everyone worries; it is a normal part of life, and at times it can be healthy. However, excessive worrying about things that you have no control over is a waste of time. For example, people worry about their past, about the mistakes they once made, and how much they wish they could go back in time and erase them.

There are several things that we are certain about in life, and one of them is that we can't go back in time—it's impossible. That's why worrying about what happened in the past is a massive waste of time and energy. You will never move forward in life if you live in your past.

Can you imagine driving a car and constantly looking in the rear-view mirror? There is a greater chance you would crash before arriving at your destination. To overcome this tendency, decide that you are going to use your past mistakes as a guide for the future by taking the lessons from them and refusing to repeat the same mistakes over and over again. Here is a short exercise to help sort out your worries:

Exercise: Get a paper and pen, divide the sheet into four sections, and write the following titles at the top of each one:

- Things I worry about
- Level of control
- How it benefits me
- Is there anything I can do?

No matter how big or small, write down all the things you are worried about in the first column. For example, you might be worried about your financial situation, your children's behavior, problems with your partner, dwelling on events in the past, etc.

In the second column, write down the degree of control you have over each problem. You can write total control, some control, or no control.

Now write down whether thinking about the problems you are worrying about benefits you in any way.

In the last column, write down whether there is anything you could do to resolve the situation. For example, if you are having problems with your partner, one solution might be couples counseling. Worrying about past events is something you can't resolve because of course, it is impossible to go back in time.

As you go through this exercise you will learn that a lot of the problems you worry about are things that you either can't control or you have very little control over. The question now becomes, 'What are you going to do about it?' You have three choices: you can either keep worrying, accept it, or do something about it. I would advise that you stop worrying about the things you can't change and start working on the things that you can. In this way, you free yourself from the anxious feelings associated with worry, knowing that you have done all you can to resolve your situation.

Complete Unfinished Business: How many entries do you have on your to-do list that you've left unchecked? Even if you've forgotten about something, unfinished business is a source of unconscious stress that hinders you from moving forward.

Exercise: Look for your old to-do lists. They are usually hidden under a messy pile on your desk. Take a pen and paper and write down everything you either have started but didn't finish, or tasks that you never got around to starting. You can take this exercise a step further and divide the list into categories such as work-related duties, daily chores, administrative tasks, etc.

Once you have written your list, decide on a day, or days when you can complete the projects. Once you have set a date, don't push them back because accumulated uncompleted tasks leave you feeling stressed and overwhelmed. Once your mind is cleared, you will increase your mental capacity, which will enable you to feel more motivated.

If you really want to overcome procrastination, you've got to have staying power. Repetition is the key to success, and if you can implement good habits consistently for 21 days, you are well on your way to overcoming procrastination for good. In the final chapter, you will solidify your learning by embarking on a 21-day challenge.

CHAPTER 11:

THE 21 DAY CRUSH PROCRASTINATION AND BOOST PRODUCTIVITY PLAN

Overcoming procrastination is about taking action. The first law of motion states that once you start moving, you will continue, so the only way you are going to get things done is by making a conscious decision to get moving!

In this chapter, you will find 15 tips to crush procrastination and boost your productivity levels. You will find that some of these tips apply to you and some don't. The idea is to read through them and see which ones will benefit you the most, and apply them for a minimum of 21 days. Once you feel you have one area under control, you can move onto to the next. Also, some of the tips don't require 21-day implementation; you do it once and keep it moving. Does that make sense? Ok—let's go!

TIP 1: CANCEL NEGATIVE PEOPLE

Negativity is like a deadly virus that affects everyone it comes into contact with. If you keep spending time in flu-ridden outbreak hotspots, eventually you are going to end up sick. The same applies to negative people. Unfortunately, we live in a world where it's easier to complain and be miserable than it is to be upbeat and happy.

You only have to turn on the TV and you are bombarded with news reports and images of the chaos we are surrounded by. Most people dislike their jobs or hate their bosses, and you are more likely to hear the latest gossip in the breakroom than hear your coworkers speak about anything motivational and uplifting.

The worst thing about negativity is that once you catch it, it festers and lingers, causing harm to your inner soul and breaking down your resolve. Unless you eradicate it from your system, it will infiltrate your thoughts, agree with your inner critic, and slowly chip away at your happiness.

As mentioned, we live in a negative world, which means we can't avoid negativity altogether. Whether we are at work, home, or traveling on public transportation, we are exposed to chronic complainers, people who always have some disaster going on in their life and have a problem for every solution. They gossip, backbite, lie, tell secrets, and they are quick to judge anyone who doesn't conform to their idea of normal.

How Negative People Encourage Procrastination

Prolonged negativity is emotionally exhausting. It stimulates destructive emotions that make you feel lethargic and fatigued. When you lack energy, you develop internal resistance against action.

Negativity is not good for your mood. Just think about how you feel when you leave the presence of a negative person. Are you walking down the street whistling with a smile on your face? No! You are probably scowling, cutting people off on the road, and zoning in on everything that irritates you about life. When you feel like this, productivity is the last thing on your mind and all you want to do is go to bed and get the day over with.

Finally, studies suggest that constant negative thoughts can have an adverse effect on how you reason, learn, and perceive. This alone should motivate you enough to walk away when the next negative person crosses your path. But as I have mentioned, it's literally impossible to ignore negative people altogether. The solution is in how you interact with them. It's important to remember that your job isn't to change them; you don't have time for that, and you've got to get your life together first. Instead, focus on vaccinating yourself against their dismal, sullen outlook.

ACTION STEPS

So now that you are fully aware of how negative people can hinder you from living your best life, your next step is to weed them out. Here are some steps to get you started:

Step 1: Identify all the negative people in your life, including friends, associates, family members, and colleagues at work.

Step 2: Put a cap on the time you spend with negative family members. You might feel guilty about doing this, but it's necessary for your survival. Most of us feel that we've got to tolerate emotionally abusive, insulting, and abrasive family members because they are blood-related.

This is a destructive thought process that will keep you bound to the wrong people and hinder your progress. I am sure you've heard the saying, "You can choose your friends, but you can't choose your family." This phrase is often used to justify why people tolerate toxic family members. Well, I use it in a different context and ask the question, *"Would you choose them as friends if they were not a part of your family?"* And most people wouldn't. If that's the case, why put up with them?

So, how do you go about distancing yourself from negative family members? This step is up to you. If you know that the family member is receptive to constructive criticism, then you can have a polite word with them. Pull the person to the side or sit down with them over coffee and let them know how you feel. In some cases, negative people have become so comfortable with being negative that they don't realize it's become a part of their character or personality. By having an honest conversation about how they are impacting others, you might encourage them to change.

Then there are the other family members who you know are totally irrational and there is no point in even trying. In cases like this, your only option is to feed them with a long-handled spoon. When they call, don't answer the phone all the time, or say you'll call back and conveniently forget. When they invite you out, say you're busy. If they turn up at your house, tell them you're just about to step out! Do you get the idea? Sooner or later they will get fed up with playing cat and mouse and leave you alone.

Step 3: Put a cap on the time you spend with negative friends and associates. Step 3 is a lot easier to do because, as you know, family is a different kettle of fish. The same rules apply as step 2. You may feel obligated to keep a friendship with the person you went to kindergarten with, but if they drain your energy with their negativity any time you're around them, it's time to say goodbye!

In most cases, when you start working on your goals and focusing on bettering yourself, negative people usually will leave the scene because they can't handle your excited talk about your new journey, but would rather sit and moan about how much they hate their husband! Remember, misery loves company, and in some cases, your friends will accuse you of being uppity now that you've decided to turn your life around.

Some act like crabs in a bucket and will try and pull you back down when they realize you are taking the road to self-improvement. But if you are determined, you will keep climbing. As with family, there are some friends that you will be able to have a heart to heart talk with and explain how you feel, and the conversation might prompt them to change as well. Then, there are others who you will need to play the long game with.

Step 4: Put a cap on the time you spend with negative co-workers. This step is most likely to be the easiest, even though you spend a lot of time with your co-workers, because in most cases, there is an unspoken rule that you are only work colleagues and nothing more. You might have an office night out or team event every once in a while, but that's as far as it goes. You don't go to each other's houses and they are not invited to important family events.

The negative co-worker might sit with you in a small office, or you might only see them during lunch breaks. Either way, when they start their negative conversations, instead of doing what you might normally do and just listening, stop them in their tracks and say, *"I am busy at the moment, I can't have this conversation right now, but is there anything else I can help you with?"* This approach lets your coworker know that you are willing to assist with business-related matters, but you are not interested in the negative conversation.

Step 5: Don't waste your time correcting negative people. If you are exposed to gossip about someone you know, just let it go. When you engage in conversation, even if it is to correct them, you are voluntarily handing over your energy to a negative situation. Instead of responding, find a way to remove yourself from the situation.

Step 6: Keep out of drama. Negative people are always going through some type of crisis and will find a way to drag you into it. They thrive on causing chaos and find it difficult to function unless they are involved in a conflict. If the negative associate asks for your opinion about one of their messy situations, refuse to comment. Likewise, if there is an argument between two friends or family members, don't try to be the mediator or take sides, just walk off and leave them to it.

Step 7: When one of your negative associates experiences a win, celebrate with them. Your positive attitude will short-circuit any of their attempts to criticize or gossip. A negative person could have won the lottery, but they will still find something to complain about.

Tip 2: Abandon Negative Self-Talk

We all have an inner critic—that evil voice that lurks in the background waiting for an opportunity to whisper words of discouragement into our ears. It tries to convince us that we are not good enough, not smart enough, or not attractive enough. And if we are thinking about doing anything outside of our comfort zone, our inner critic will quickly let us know that we might as well not bother trying because we are going to fail.

Negative self-talk can wreak havoc on our productivity. It shows up in different forms. For example, perfectionism is sometimes an expression of negative self-talk because the thought process of a perfectionist is that anything less than the best is failure. People who think like this find it difficult to take action.

Another sign of negative self-talk is catastrophizing, which is when a person believes that total chaos is always waiting around the corner. The fear of disaster striking causes people who think like this not to take action because they are going to do such a bad job that they will bring on the disaster.

Polarizing is another example of our inner critic at work. It is a tendency to see everything as black or white. There is no grey area. People who think in this way see themselves as either right or wrong, successful or hopeless, attractive or ugly, dumb or smart.

HOW NEGATIVE SELF TALK ENCOURAGES PROCRASTINATION

Negative self-talk is like a horrible friend who doesn't want you to succeed. Your inner critic waits for the slightest hint of doubt and then encourages it until you are consumed with fear. When you do feel a spark of positivity, the voice will quickly put your fire out. At this point, every task becomes a massive burden over-shadowed by a cloud of potential failure. You become terrified of taking responsibility because your inner critic has convinced you that it will end in disaster.

It's impossible to be productive when you think this way about yourself and your abilities. It paralyzes you with doubt and the fear that any action taken will prove your inner critic right.

ACTION STEPS

The good news is that you can drown out the voice of your inner critic. Once you develop some new habits, you will find it a lot easier to take purposeful action in every area of your life.

Step 1 - Recognize Your Inner Critic: Pay attention to the things your inner critic is saying about you and take note of how it makes you feel. At first, you will find it difficult to connect with a voice that conjures up so many negative emotions—this is normal. However, the more you focus on it, the easier it will become to recognize the voice.

Step 2 - Remind Yourself That It's Not True: Tell yourself that your inner critic is nothing but a liar. When you confront the voice, and ask for evidence, you will find that it has none. For example, let's say you plan on going to a social event and your inner critic tells you there is no point in going because the people who are going to be there don't like you. When you ask for evidence, and you are reminded of the friends you have, it will become clear that what the voice is saying isn't true. Don't be afraid to let your inner critic know that you know it's a liar.

Step 3 - Reframe Your Thoughts: Reframe your negative thinking so that your thoughts are unprejudiced and impartial. For example, let's say your boss gives you an unfamiliar task to complete. Your inner critic is going to say something like, *"You will never be able to do that; you are not experienced in it."* Respond with, *"It might be a challenge, but I will give it my best shot."*

Step 4 - Document Your Inner Critic: Since your inner critic is incapable of gathering evidence against you because nothing it says is true, start collecting evidence against your inner critic! This will come in the form of writing down everything that it says about you. Keep these writings so that every time you experience a win over your inner critic, you can let the voice know that it was wrong.

Step 5 – Become Your Number One Fan: When I was younger, I was a massive Michael Jackson fan, and if anyone said anything bad about him, I would kindly let them know why he was the best musician in the world. This is the job of a number one fan; they are there to silence the critics! When that silent voice rises up and starts whispering all manner of evil into your ear, respond with something positive. For example, when it says: *"You are the worst public speaker on the planet, no one is ever going to hire you!"* Respond with, *"Actually, I'm pretty good; and for your information, you are the only person who has said I'm not!"* Whatever negative attributes your inner critic tries to highlight, silence it by pointing out all of your positive attributes.

Step 6 – Develop a Growth Mindset: Psychologist Carol Dweck's studies on mindset found that there are two dominant mindsets: the "fixed mindset" and the "growth mindset." When you are under the influence of your inner critic, you are operating with a fixed mindset. The fixed mindset is one that believes there is no room for self-improvement.

If you don't have the right skills to get a better job, you will remain in your current employment forever, or there is no point in trying to lose weight, this is just the way you are. On the other hand, a growth mindset sees an opportunity in every negative situation. It is a 'can-do' mindset that advocates for self-improvement and believes anything is possible for the person who is determined.

To develop a growth mindset, you've got to constantly challenge the fixed mindset in words and actions. The voice of your inner critic loses its power the more you achieve the things that it says you can't.

Tip 3: Conduct Weekly Reviews

Productivity is about making progress. If you don't measure productivity, you will end up getting stuck in a rut. One of the main reasons for this is that sometimes we can look productive but, really, we aren't doing much. This syndrome appears in the form of writing to-do lists and preparing for what we need to do without actually doing it. The only way to overcome the stagnation is to monitor your progress to see how effective you have been.

When you look back on everything you set out to achieve for the week, did you get everything done or were certain things left unfinished? If you didn't manage to get everything done, what was the reason? Sometimes the reasons are legitimate, but most of the time it's because we've been procrastinating. Once you've determined what you didn't get done, the next step is to work out how you are going to prioritize those things the following week.

Weekly reviews are often frowned upon, especially in the workplace where employees feel that their bosses are micromanaging them. But some people neglect to do them simply because they don't know how to go about it. They recognize the value in appraising their weekly performance, but they don't know how to go about it.

How Failing to Conduct Weekly Reviews Encourages Procrastination

Whether at work or home, we are always on the go, and sometimes it can feel as if there are not enough hours in the day to get everything done. It's no wonder we feel exhausted and frazzled mid-week and can't wait until the weekend. But for those of us with kids, life can often get even more hectic on the weekends!

Without conducting weekly reviews, it's difficult to identify the obstacles that are crippling our productivity. For example, did you agree to take on more responsibilities than your availability would allow? Did you agree to attend social events with friends or meetings at work that cut into your other obligations? Did you create a to-do list as long as your arm and set yourself up for failure? Did you fall behind on emails, bills, and paperwork and neglect important relationships because you were dealing with issues that could have been avoided if you had planned better?

Everyone has their flaws when it comes to work, and there is always room for improvement. When we improve our approach to work both at home and on the job, we feel more in control and organized. We feel empowered! It also gives us extra time to do the things that are important to us.

Action Steps

Conducting weekly reviews is extremely valuable. It teaches us how to optimize our processes and helps us to get more work done in less time. If you are not sure how to go about conducting a weekly review, here are some steps to follow:

Step 1 - Set a Timeframe: A review should be short and sweet; it shouldn't take you all day. Remember, you are trying to generate more time, not waste it. Therefore, your weekly review shouldn't take you more than 30 minutes.

Step 2 – Put it on Your Calendar: This will train your mind to see your weekly review as an action item, meaning you are less likely to disregard it. Select a day and time that works best for you and stick to it. For example, a good day and time is Sunday at 7 pm. The week is over, and you are preparing to start another week.

Step 3 - Review Uncompleted Tasks: Review projects and chores that you didn't manage to complete that week. Why couldn't you get to them? Did you underestimate how long they would take? Did you agree to do things that you shouldn't have? Did you lack focus or were you procrastinating? Did you spend too much time scrolling through social media? Once you have identified the problem, make sure you don't make the same mistakes the next week.

Step 4 - What Went Well: It's easy to get caught up with the things that didn't go as planned, but what about the things that *did* go well? What tasks did you manage to complete? What were the strategies you used that helped you get things done? Did you turn your phone off when it was time to work on a project? Did you say no to the people you would usually say yes to? Did you install a site blocker on your browser to prevent you from spending countless hours surfing the internet? Did you wake up an hour earlier and work on personal things before making your way to the office? Once you find out what works for you, rinse and repeat.

Step 5 - Maintain a Zero Inbox: Accumulated email is a constant source of stress for many of us; the best way to avoid this stressor is to get rid of them. During your weekly review, organize your emails. Resist the temptation to reply to all of them and only reply to the emails that you consider urgent, store the ones you can reply to at a later date in a folder, and delete the rest. Your aim is to have no messages in your inbox.

Step 6 – Plan Your Week on Your Calendar: What projects do you need to complete this week? Make a list of high-priority and low-priority tasks. During this step, if you realize that you didn't give yourself enough time to complete certain tasks last week, give yourself more time to complete them this week.

TIP 4: TIME OUT

"I don't have time for a vacation, I've got too much to do" Do these words sound familiar to you? Most of us spend plenty of time daydreaming about dropping everything and relaxing for a week. But unfortunately, for most of us, getting away from the busyness of our lives and the stresses of our jobs is just that—a dream! On the other hand, when we are offered a vacation, instead of breathing a sigh of relief, we hesitate and start calculating the potential consequences of taking time off. Will our career suffer? What about our home and social/civic/religious obligations?

In the United States, people are not fond of going on long breaks. Research suggests that Americans often forfeit their vacation days and prefer to rack up the extra pay at work instead. But this issue isn't relegated to Americans alone, it appears to be a human problem. Data compiled by the United Kingdom's Office of National Statistics suggests that English workers don't like using all their holiday time either.

Failing to unplug and take the time out to relax has two major consequences. First, it's detrimental to our health and well-being; and second, over time, it can disrupt our productivity.

How Failing to Relax Encourages Procrastination

Busyness at the office, in your social life, and at home causes mental exhaustion. The constant need to make decisions chips away at our cognitive resources, which leaves us feeling irritable, apathetic, stressed, and emotionally drained. Eventually, these conditions will affect our ability to work efficiently. We will find it extremely difficult to focus, lose motivation to complete important tasks, and ultimately betray our convictions to work in a way that's consistent with our standards. Many of us silently congratulate ourselves for our work ethic and perseverance, although our workaholic ways threaten to undermine our productivity completely.

It might appear as if you are coping with the stresses of everyday life because you have learned to deal with them in your own way. However, the damage it is causing is invisible until a life-threatening illness comes knocking at your door. Not to be the bearer of bad news, but did you know that the majority of people die prematurely because of stress-related illnesses?

The solution is to unplug by taking a long vacation. On the surface, it makes no sense: you've got so much to do, you haven't cleared the deck at work, you've got to take care of the kids, etc. But what you will find is that going on vacation is like recharging your batteries. The human body is like your cell phone. If you keep using it without charging the battery, eventually it will die. When you take a break, you are refueling so that when you return, you will have even more energy and determination than you had before, which will boost your productivity.

ACTION STEPS

Not sure how to make it happen? Keep reading!

Step 1 - Pick a Date: There is no point in waiting for the right conditions—your work, home, and social life will never be in perfect alignment. There is always going to be a project, a task, and an activity that requires your attention. If you wait for the perfect window of opportunity to magically appear on your calendar, you'll be waiting for an eternity. Don't let the perfect be the enemy of the good. The only way to do it is by scheduling time off well ahead and then letting others know about your plans.

Step 2 - Get Stuff Done: Make a list of every task, project, and meeting, both at work and at home that requires your attention. Schedule time on your calendar to complete these items during the weeks leading up to your vacation. One of the main reasons people don't like taking time off is because they are afraid of neglecting important tasks. You can overcome this concern by getting them done before you leave. You may need to get up a couple of hours earlier or go to bed a couple of hours later, but your main aim should be to complete everything on your to-do list so you can enjoy your vacation without worrying about the things you need to do when you get home.

Step 3 - Don't Work on Your Vacation: The main aim of going on a vacation is to completely detach yourself from work life. If you are checking your emails and working on projects then you haven't detached or unplugged, and you are not on vacation. In fact, don't even bring your laptop with you.

Step 4 - Plan Time off Around Company Holidays: All establishments take time off no matter how busy they are. Let's say your office is going to be closed on a Monday. Take time off on the Friday before, as well as the following Tuesday and Wednesday. The idea is to take a break when your presence is not as important as usual.

Step 5 - Ask at the Right Time: Some people are hesitant to ask their employers for time off; this is especially true if you are considered an asset to your company. The good news is that there are tactics you can implement to simplify the process. First, don't ask for time off during peak periods. Second, do ask for time off via email so that you've got a paper trail. Third, give as much notice as possible so that management has enough time to prepare for your absence. Fourth, ask your manager when it would be most convenient to take time off; this way, you put the ball in their court. If you've got a project to complete, suggest dates as soon as it's completed. Fifth, make your manager's job easier and come up with a plan for how your workload will get divided among your co-workers (make sure you get permission from them first). Once you've got everything organized, then ask your boss for a vacation. When you present your case in a package like this, it will be extremely difficult for your boss to say no.

Step 6 - Plan a Staycation: You don't need to travel halfway across the world and spend thousands of dollars to go on vacation. Remember, the main aim of taking a break is to sever the connection between you and your normal chaotic routine of responsibilities. You can accomplish this goal at home, as long as you stick to the plan of not working. You can even plan on visiting a few local places you've never been to before. The benefits of taking a staycation are that you will save money, you already know how to get around town, and you can take full advantage of the personal comforts you are already accustomed to.

TIP 5: START WAKING UP EARLY

Most of us envy the rich and successful, scratching our heads as to how they managed to achieve such a high level of prosperity. The assumption is that the only reason there is such a small handful of wealthy people is because they have access to resources the rest of the world don't have, or they've got some superhuman strength. None of this is true. The reality is that highly successful people do things that the rest of us are not willing to do. And one of them is that they wake up early.

The average person thinks there isn't enough time in the day to get things done. That is not the issue—it's what you choose to do with your time that counts. One of the main differences between rich people and average people is how they manage their time, and it starts by waking up early.

Remember, the CEO of Starbucks Howard Schultz, Richard Branson of Virgin, and Tim Cook of Apple all wake up early and accredit their success in part to this important habit.

However, the average person hits the snooze button ten times before they are forced to get out of bed an hour before they've got to be at work. They then spend the first part of their day rushing around getting ready and end up running through the door with seconds (or no time at all) to spare.

How Does Waking up Late Encourage Procrastination

First, people who wake up late don't get good quality sleep (which is essential for productivity). The reason for this is that when you don't have a regular sleep pattern, it affects your circadian rhythm (your internal clock), and this prevents you from enjoying a restful night. For example, have you ever gone to bed in the early hours of the morning because you spent the night binge-watching your favorite show on Netflix? As a result, you woke up late the following morning and felt disorientated and woozy because you disrupted your sleep/wake cycle.

It is virtually impossible to be productive when you intercept your circadian rhythm because it causes the brain to send conflicting signals to the body. Without getting too scientific, one of the consequences is that your brain starts releasing melatonin at the wrong time. Melatonin is the chemical that lets your body know it's time to go to bed, and this is typically released at night.

Second, waking up late because of irregular sleep habits causes you to feel lethargic. Getting out of bed later than you intended hampers your enthusiasm for the day. You feel listless, disorientated and anxious because you know certain things are not going to get done because you don't have the time.

Action Steps

If you feel like you are stuck in a rut because you keep waking up late, you can resolve the situation by implementing a few techniques. I'm not saying it's going to be easy because breaking out of bad habits is never easy. But if you are consistent and determined, you can do it.

Step 1 - Go to Bed at the Same Time Every Night: Decide what time to go to bed and stick to it. Resist the temptation to binge-watch your favorite shows on Netflix, getting into a debate on social media, or watching comedy skits on YouTube.

Step 2 - Pick a Wake-up Time and Stick to it: Never sleep in—EVER! Not even on the weekends! These are the steps you will need to take to reset your circadian rhythm. If you wake up later on the weekends, you will confuse your body.

Step 3 - Avoid Caffeine and Alcohol: Caffeine is a no brainer because that's what most of us drink during the day to keep us awake. However, alcohol is not so obvious. The assumption is that alcohol helps you sleep better. Research suggests that alcohol prevents us from entering into the deep sleep phase of delta waves. Now you know why you feel so groggy in the morning when you've had a few glasses of wine before going to bed. Although it helps you fall asleep faster, it also interferes with deep sleep.

Step 4 - Put Your Alarm Clock in Another Room: The aim here is to force you to get out of bed. When your alarm clock is on the nightstand next to you, as soon as it goes off, you stretch out your hand and hit the snooze button. If it's in another room, you'll need to get up and move to turn it off. Once you've gotten out of bed, you will find it much easier to get on with your day.

Step 5 - Have a Plan: Most of us go to work first thing in the morning, whether you work from home or you commute. But it also helps to have a morning routine. This might include going to the gym, reading, meditating, or journaling. Whatever it is, these plans give us a reason to get out of bed on time instead of giving in to the temptation to pull the cover over our heads and go back to sleep.

Tip 6: Stop Responding to Voicemails, Texts, and Emails

I believe one of the reasons this generation suffers from disorders such as ADHD is because there are so many distractions. Just take a trip to the store and people watch for an hour or so and you will learn very quickly that we are obsessed with our phones. The problem is that technology is now so advanced that everything we need is available at the click of a button we can pull out of our pockets. We can check our email, and go online from our phone, and anytime it demands our attention, we run to its rescue as if we are responding to the cries of a hungry baby! The problem is that most of us are bombarded with messages, and once we respond to one, we respond to the others and before we know it, everything we were supposed to do has gone out the window!

How Responding to Messages Immediately Encourages Procrastination

The main problem with responding to messages immediately is the interruption it causes. Replying to a quick email might seem insignificant because it only takes up five minutes of our time, but the problem is that it hinders our ability to focus. Research suggests that it takes the brain approximately 20 minutes to get back on track after an interruption. That's a lot of time wasted that could have been spent completing your tasks.

The second problem is that when you respond right away to messages, it gives the sender the impression that you are always available, and they will expect the same quick response every time they contact you. It might be an unspoken rule, but then when you don't respond as quickly as you normally do, the sender wonder why. Eventually, you will get frustrated with the demands placed on you to respond to messages immediately.

ACTION STEPS

If you've fallen into the habit of being glued to your phone every time you get a message, it's time to put a stop to it!

Step 1 - Forget About Etiquette: Your happiness and well-being are more important than anything. If you are going to make positive changes in your life, you will need to stop people-pleasing. Stop being concerned about what your friends or family members are going to think if you don't respond to their messages immediately. Forget about how your coworkers will feel if you don't reply within five minutes of receiving an email or text message. Everyone has different digital etiquette rules. Don't live according to everyone else's standards, live according to yours. And think about proper etiquette involving the people who are with you *in person*. They matter just as much or more.

Step 2 - Check Your Emails Twice Per Day: Select two times, for example 12:00 p.m. and 5:00 p.m., and stick to them. Fight the temptation to respond to emails outside of those windows. As mentioned, technology has made it easier to access our emails. Once upon a time, we could only reply to emails if we had access on a work or home computer. If not, we had to go to an internet café or the local library. So back then, no one responded to emails immediately.

Step 3 - Respond to Texts Twice a Day: Apply the same rules as step 2. Choose two times during the day and stick to them. In my opinion, it makes more sense to respond to emails and messages at the same time. It's a similar activity, so it makes sense to batch them, which will also save time. You will find it hard to respond to messages twice a day at first because it's not what you're accustomed to. If something is urgent, the person can call you and leave a voice message if you can't pick up.

If you stick with this plan, you will realize how beneficial it is and you will realize that it's a huge advantage in your life. Most people will learn to accept that this is your new normal and they'll have to wait to hear back from you. Unfortunately, some of your friends, family members, and coworkers will convince themselves that you are being disrespectful and will feel snubbed.

Remember, that's their problem and not yours. The only way to soften the blow a bit is to warn them about your intentions in advance. You should also speak to your boss about this subject because there may be a chance that it's not conducive to your workflow. But if it is, you should inform your coworkers as well.

If your job requires that you check messages throughout the day, apply a GTD protocol (Getting Things Done), where you look at each message once and decide immediately what you are going to do with it. For example, your boss might send a message that requires you to respond right away. But the message from your colleague might not require any action at all, meaning that you can just archive it. A voicemail from a vendor or client might require that you follow up after finding out certain information. You can arrange to call them back once you've got the information on hand. Of course, this situation isn't ideal, but if you don't have any other choice, you can streamline interruptions using a GTD protocol.

TIP 7: ELIMINATE DISTRACTIONS

Distractions are the biggest productivity killers. Most of the time, they are so subtle, we don't even realize we have been distracted until it's too late. Distractions prey upon our desire to avoid work. Let's face it, none of us always want to work. It's human nature to want to take the path of least resistance. Most of us would rather engage in leisure activities than spend eight hours a day cooped up in an office.

How many times have you found yourself visiting YouTube, Facebook, or news websites while you should be working? It's almost as if the brain actively looks for stimuli to distract it. Once we are distracted, we lose momentum and it's difficult to get back on track. In some cases, we decide to stop working altogether and and surrender to the distractions.

HOW DISTRACTIONS ENCOURAGE PROCRASTINATION

There are several ways that distractions hinder productivity. First, they weaken your focus when you are working on something that requires your undivided attention, and you've really gotten into the flow of things. A single distraction can completely knock you off course, and you will then find it even more difficult to get back into the 'flow' because of how intense your focus was.

Second, distraction has a negative effect on the overall quality of your work. When you work without interruption, it is easier to produce high-quality output. Due to broken focus, the task will take a lot longer to complete than it normally would, and increase the likelihood of making mistakes.

Third, distractions make you less patient. The more your productivity declines, the more frustrated you will become. Continuous distractions will eventually take a toll on your mood. You will find it increasingly difficult to deal with adverse conditions, and you will become more and more aggravated at things you would otherwise have taken with a grain of salt.

Fourth, distractions actually make you forgetful. Have you ever become distracted by one thing only to find that you forget about the task you were originally working on?

And finally, distractions make us less attentive. Some people claim to be great multitaskers (you might be one of them). However, research suggests that multitasking makes you 40% less productive. Another study found that just thinking about multitasking led to a reduced IQ similar to that caused by mental distress after losing a night's sleep.

ACTION STEPS

When I made the decision to 10X my life and really go for what I wanted, I discovered that people were my biggest distraction. Friends, family members, and loved ones often feel that they have a right to your time and attention. You will find that many people get offended when you initiate these action steps. However, that's not your problem. If you are going to get anywhere in life, you must be able to focus on reaching your goals. So here are some steps you can take to eliminate distractions.

Step 1 – Switch Off Your Devices: Unfortunately, many of us find it difficult to live without our phones. I would go as far as to say that we have become a nation of people addicted to the "ping." As soon as we hear that sound, we start scrambling to check our messages as if we are going to miss out on something if we don't know everything that's going on in the world. The most effective way to deal with this is simply to switch off your devices, and if you are working from a tablet or an iPhone, turn off your notifications.

Step 2 – Close Your Browsers: Sometimes it's not people who distract you the most, it's you! Have you ever found when working on certain projects you have different browsers open for your favorite websites, whether it's a shopping site or a blog, and you keep flicking between them anytime you feel the urge? This is one of the many ways your focus is broken. However, you can avoid this problem by closing down any browser not related to the task at hand.

Step 3 – Learn to Recognize the Signs of Distraction: There are several telltale signs that let you know when you are about to become distracted. You start thinking about something else, you will stop what you are doing and start daydreaming, or you decide that you need a drink or a sandwich, even though you are not hungry or thirsty. Once you realize that these thoughts and feelings are a form of distraction, you can start working to overcome them.

Step 4 – Remember Why You Are Doing it: When that feeling of distraction rears its ugly head, remind yourself why you are working on that particular task. Stop, take a deep breath and think about your goals. For example, if you have an exam in a couple of weeks, remind yourself that you've got to study if you want to pass. If you are cleaning your house, remind yourself that you are having dinner guests the next evening. Whatever you are working toward, remind yourself and that should motivate you to keep going.

Step 5 – Practice Working on Your Focus: Concentration is like a muscle. Therefore, exercise it by engaging in activities that improve your ability to focus such as meditation, reading long-form articles, and listening to educational content.

Step 6 - Prepare for the Distractions: Let your friends, family members, co-workers, and loved ones know that you will be unavailable during certain times. Any rational person will respect your boundaries. By preparing for the distractions in this way, you are eliminating them before they happen. Good preparation increases your chances of success.

TIP 8: BECOME EMOTIONALLY INDEPENDENT

I believe that this is a deeper issue, and, in some cases, you may need professional help to conquer it. However, for those who don't, it can be dealt with by following the steps I will outline below. Many people depend on others for emotional support— to a certain extent there is nothing wrong with this, we are all emotional creatures and need support from others especially when things aren't going too well.

However, this becomes a problem when we are completely dependent on others to make us happy and to feel secure. As a result, we find it difficult to be alone. If we can't be with someone physically, we will spend hours on the phone having fruitless conversations just to feel uplifted, happy, or to seek validation. Emotional dependency also leads to people ending up in unhealthy relationships.

All of this encourages procrastination. Why? Because instead of working on the important stuff, you are either staring at your phone waiting for it to ring, jumping in the car to visit that person you depend on, or spending hours on the phone talking rubbish to fill that void.

When your emotional state is dependent upon another person, you forget about yourself, and you put all your time and energy into pleasing that person because you don't want to lose their favor. Emotional dependency not only takes place in romantic relationships, but it also takes place among family members, friends, and co-workers. In some cases, our interactions with complete strangers can impact our emotions to the point that we feel distressed and dejected.

HOW EMOTIONAL DEPENDENCY ENCOURAGES PROCRASTINATION

One of the symptoms of emotional dependency is anxiety—the result of your constant need to receive validation from the person you are emotionally dependent upon. Anxiety has a negative effect on productivity. It is impossible to concentrate when you are drowning in insecurity and fear, and when you can't focus, the quality of your work and your performance will suffer.

Anger is another symptom of emotional dependency. People experience anger when the person we are emotionally dependent upon fails to respond the way we want. Even if the person is not trying to reject us, we assume they are. Anger is not only distracting, but it is exhausting and makes it impossible to concentrate. On a deeper level, continuous feelings of aggravation can drain your willpower and energy, leaving you with limited reserves to work productively.

When you are emotionally dependent on someone, you almost become obsessed with that person. Whether you are stalking them on social media or waiting for them to contact you, these negative feelings take control of your mind, and it adversely affects your behavior, leading you to neglect the things that matter the most.

ACTION STEPS

The main aim of these action steps is to release yourself from the need to rely on others for your emotional health. Once you become emotionally self-reliant, you will free up your mental resources so that you can focus on the things that are most important to you.

Step 1 - Create Something for Yourself: If you play an instrument, compose a song and share it with no one. If you cook, create a recipe and keep it to yourself, or write a journal containing your deepest secrets. Whatever creative activity you choose, it belongs to you, so don't share it with anyone; neither should you tell anyone about it. The point is to have something that represents your creativity and makes you happy, which you can return to anytime you start feeling emotionally dependent.

Step 2 - Have Alone Time: Seek out exciting activities you can enjoy alone; for example, take a walk-through nature on your own, grab your favorite book and go to Starbucks, or have a meal alone at your favorite restaurant. The purpose of alone time is to learn how to enjoy your own company.

Step 3 - Learn a New Skill: Is there a skill you would like to learn? Dancing, learning to play a musical instrument or to edit your own pictures with photoshop might be just the thing.

Learning new things increases self-confidence. As your ability with your new skill increases and you start feeling better about yourself, you will feel less emotionally dependent on others.

Step 4 - Personal Development: Whatever capacity you choose to improve yourself in will take time and energy. Whether you are learning how to make better decisions, manage stress, listen actively, or improve your communication skills, you will have no room in your life for emotional dependency because of your laser focus on yourself. Once you realize that you are the author of your own success, you will stop relying on other people.

Step 5 - Accept Responsibility for Your Emotional Well-Being: No one can affect your emotions unless you allow them to. For example, if you are angry, recognize that you feel this way because of your perception of the situation and not because of someone else. If you are lonely, understand that your loneliness is because you have chosen to rely on other people to feel fulfilled instead of being fulfilled from within. If you are anxious, your anxiety is not caused by others, so accept that it actually comes from within.

Step 6 - Make Decisions for Yourself: Emotionally dependent people have a bad habit of seeking approval from others instead of doing what feels right to them. If they want to write a book, they will ask a friend what they think; if they want to cut their hair, they need the approval of someone before they go ahead and do it. I am not suggesting that you shouldn't seek advice from others. However, it is important that you know what you want out of life and go for it rather than wait for others to give you the green light.

There is no denying that taking responsibility for your emotional state is easier said than done, and it's not going to happen overnight. However, if you are consistent in taking small steps, you will get there eventually.

TIP 9: STOP ACCEPTING MEDIOCRITY

Many people never achieve what they truly want out of life. They set low goals for themselves and put the least amount of effort into achieving them. This is the case in careers, relationships, personal lives, etc. Despite the underlying feeling of disappointment in life, the majority of people accept this existence because it is easier. The bottom line is that success requires hard work. There is not one person on the planet who has achieved a massive amount of success without sweat, blood and tears for it. It is normal for humans to want to take the path of least resistance, self-discipline doesn't feel good at first. I for one would rather lie in bed and watch Netflix on the weekend instead of waking up at 5 am to work on my goals. However, I am determined to live my dreams, so I know that I've got to make sacrifices to achieve them.

The biggest issue with settling for mediocrity is that once you have accepted it, it becomes a normal part of your life. Eventually, you forget about your goals and dreams and settle for the status quo. The problem is that the majority of people settle, and it's likely the people you are surrounded by share the same mindset.

HOW SETTLING FOR MEDIOCRITY ENCOURAGES PROCRASTINATION

It's easy to get stuck in a rut when we are willing to settle for mediocrity. How many of you reading this have set the same goal year after year but you still haven't accomplished it?

Most people never challenge themselves and never step outside their comfort zone and, therefore, never achieve anything worthwhile. Settling for mediocrity leads to sacrificing professional and personal goals and we miss opportunities to broaden our knowledge and expand our skillset. Just think about how much more you could contribute to those around you and the world at large if you were operating at your highest potential?

Accepting mediocrity causes us to lose sight of our weaknesses, and we develop tunnel vision that obscures our reality. Our weaknesses are dismissed as irrelevant because they are not contributing to what we are currently doing. Because we are not pursuing personal growth, we don't see these things as urgent. So as the world keeps advancing, we remain the same, which means we are unable to take advantage of the opportunities that present themselves.

Have you ever wanted a promotion at work and someone else got it? Or witnessed what happens when someone gets a promotion? The people who were overlooked become extremely jealous and start lobbing all types of accusations against the person who got the promotion. I am not denying that sometimes people are promoted for no reason other than who they know.

However, some people are constantly striving to be the best versions of themselves. You won't witness them doing anything out of the ordinary; but after work, they go home and read books, or they might be taking a course, but they do the things required to become an expert and it shows when they are in the office. In other words, the things that are done in private, are rewarded publicly, and when you live a life of mediocrity, that causes jealousy. Deep down you want more and resent others who have the discipline required to go after what they want.

Action Steps

If you are tired of living in the valley and want to know what life is like at the mountain top, put these action steps to work and watch your productivity soar!

Step 1 – Visualize: What do you want out of life? Close your eyes and imagine that you have it. Deep down most people know exactly what they want, but they are afraid of failure, so they never attempt to work toward it.

Step 2 – Get a Mentor or Coach: The fastest way to become successful is to get a mentor or a coach. Every successful person had a mentor before they became successful, and they still have a mentor now. Oprah Winfrey was mentored by Maya Angelou; Tiger Woods was mentored by Joe Grohman; and Michael Jordan was mentored by Dean Smith. A mentor or coach who has been in your shoes and knows how to get where you want to go will know exactly how to push you in the right direction.

Step 3 – Make a Promise to Yourself: Make a promise that you are going to do your best with everything—and I mean EVERYTHING! How you wash the dishes, iron your clothes, make your bed, or wash your car counts. Make excellence your standard in every area of life and it will become the norm.

Step 4 - Be Willing to do What Others Won't: Be that person in the office, at home, or at school who is always volunteering to do the things that no one else wants to do. First, it will get you used to stepping out of your comfort zone. Second, people will begin to respect you for your tenacity; and third, you will start inspiring people to do more than they would usually do.

Step 5 - Cut Down Your TV Watching Time: There is nothing wrong with watching television. The problem is that people watch too much of it. After a long day at work, it feels great to unwind with your favorite TV show. However, our original intention is always to watch one or two episodes before moving on to more important things. But in most cases, we end up binge-watching programs and falling asleep on the sofa. We then promise ourselves that we will start working on the project tomorrow, the same thing happens, and we end up in a vicious cycle.

You can start by reviewing all the shows you are currently watching, choose the one you are not too concerned about and stop watching it. Do the same the next week, and then the week after that until you have reduced the amount of TV you watch by 50%.

TIP 10: MAKE DECISIONS QUICKLY

The faster you make a decision, the more quickly you are going to take action. Indecision is a form of procrastination because you are not going to do anything when you are uncertain of what to do. There are several reasons you might find it difficult to make a decision.

Too Many Options: When you are getting ready for a night out and you've got 20 outfits to choose from, it's going to take you longer to get ready than if you had only three outfits to choose from. The fewer choices you have, the faster you will make a decision.

Laziness: When you feel sluggish and tired, the last thing you want to do is make a decision because you know that once you have made a decision, your next step is to take action.

Perfectionism: Perfectionists struggle with decision making because they don't want to take the risk of failing. The underlying thought process is that if I never start, I won't know what it feels like to fail and then end up depressed because it wasn't perfect.

Fear of Taking Ownership: When you make a decision it belongs to you, no one made the choice for you. Therefore, you own whatever consequences are attached to that decision. Some people don't like taking responsibility for their actions and will avoid making decisions because of this attribution.

A Lack of Purpose: When you don't know what you want out of life, and you have no clear goals or values, it's difficult to make decisions. People who have a clear view of where they are going typically make decisions based on their main goal.

How Indecisiveness Encourages Procrastination

Indecisiveness could be one of the worst habits to destroy your productivity. First, it erodes your self-confidence. Each time you struggle to make a decision, your inner critic gains ground and uses it as ammunition to attack your confidence. The more it happens, the worse you feel about yourself.

Second, overthinking things causes you to miss out on opportunities. For example, let's say you are given the chance to work on an important project at work, but instead of rising to the challenge, you take too long to think about it. Eventually, the opportunity is given to someone else. Due to your indecisiveness, you miss the chance to enhance your skills and meet key people within your organization.

Third, indecisiveness is a big-time waster. According to Parkinson's Law, the more time we have to work on something, the more time we take to do it. If you find it difficult to make decisions, time will continue to evade you, and everything you do will take longer than necessary.

Fourth, it hinders your working memory, which is like a computer's RAM (random access memory). This is where your mind temporarily stores information to process it later. Like a computer's RAM, working memory is in limited supply. The problem is, the more options you have to choose from the longer it takes to make a decision and this causes stress and pressure. Studies reveal that stress and pressure are detrimental to your working memory, leaving you with limited resources to process information.

ACTION STEPS

If you struggle with indecision, you know how badly it affects your productivity; but not to worry, here are some tips to assist you with the decision-making process.

Step 1 – Accept That You Will Need to Sacrifice Something: One of the reasons we don't like making decisions is because we fear we are going to miss out on something. For example, there are two movies you want to watch, but you've only got time to see one of them. This dilemma can cause you to waste time weighing up your options when your circumstances will only allow you to watch one film. Once you accept that it's impossible to have everything, it will become easier for you to make decisions quickly.

Step 2 – Stop Spending so Much Time on Research: There is nothing wrong with wanting to make an intelligent decision. The more you know about something the easier it will be for you to decide. However, it is impossible to find out every last detail about something. Get enough information to enable you to make a comparison, then make your decision and keep it moving.

Step 3 - Give Yourself a Time Limit: The time limit you give yourself will depend on the weightiness of the decision. When you put a deadline on something, it will force you to make a decision.

Step 4 - Accept That You Will Make Some Bad Decisions: It isn't always possible to make the right decision. Even if you have investigated the situation as much as you can and made your choice wisely, there is always the chance that something could go wrong. For example, you choose to go to a restaurant with your partner based on a friend's recommendation. You also go online and read the reviews, and no one seems to have a bad word to say about the place.

However, things are different when you get there. The staff is rude, the food is bland and to top it off, you end up with food poisoning! Your bad experience wasn't because you made the wrong decision, but because there were factors that were beyond your control that contributed to your negative experience.

Step 5 - Deal with Your Most Difficult Decisions First: Decision-making drains our willpower, and we only have a limited amount of it. Therefore, you will find it easier to make difficult decisions if you make them first thing in the morning instead of waiting until the end of the day when you are drained and tired.

Have you noticed that simple decisions such as what movie to watch, whether to go to the gym, or what to cook are harder to make at the end of the day? Getting difficult decisions out of the way first thing in the morning will help you to avoid "paralysis by analysis." It will enable you to make intelligent decisions quickly so that you can move on with your day.

Step 6 – Train Yourself to Make Quick Decisions: The aim is for fast decision-making to become a habit. You can start by making small decisions that have minor consequences quickly. Once you get used to this, move on to bigger decisions.

Tip 11: Stop Seeking Instant Gratification

When we want something, we usually want it immediately and we are not prepared to wait for it. If we have no other option than to wait, we will wait, but if we are given the choice to experience gratification now or in the future, most of us are going to choose the present. For example, suppose you could choose to eat your favorite meal now or next week and there are no consequences attached to choosing to eat it now, would you eat it now, right?

When there are no consequences attached to our actions, we are going to choose instant gratification. However, the reality is that everything you do has a consequence attached to it and there is no escape from that. Wherever you are in life is because of the choices you have made. For example, if you choose to sleep instead of going to the gym, don't expect to get into shape. If you chose to watch TV instead of study for your exams, don't be surprised when you fail to get the grades you were hoping for.

The problem is that too many people are addicted to the lure of instant gratification, they find it exceptionally difficult to resist and will pursue what they want despite the consequences.

How Instant Gratification Encourages Procrastination

Instant gratification is a form of self-sabotage. First, it steals your time so you don't have the time to focus on the things that are most important to you. If you choose to spend your time talking on the phone when you've got an exam to prepare for, you won't have enough time to study. If you choose to watch television instead of doing household chores, your house will remain a mess. We can buy most things in life, but time is something that we can never reclaim; once it's gone, we can't get it back.

Second, giving in to instant gratification encourages impulsiveness. It trains the brain to choose short-term pleasures over long-term benefits. Over time, you will develop a habit that will eventually erode your resilience and self-discipline. We find it too difficult to stick to our aspirations and goals and instead surrender to our impulses when we are confronted with a challenge.

Third, the result of giving in to your immediate urges ultimately is dissatisfaction with life. While whatever you are indulging in might make you feel good in the present moment, the result is unhappiness later on. When you look back and realize that you have failed to achieve anything you set out to because of your unproductive behaviors, a feeling of depression sets in.

Action Steps

If you are constantly giving in to the pull of instant gratification, now is the time to put this bad habit behind you and start taking control over your impulses. You will find that delaying your short-term urges will boost your productivity, help you make better decisions, and increase your resilience to hurdles as you pursue your goals.

Step 1 - What Are Your Temptations: What are the temptations that threaten to sabotage your goals? For example, you might find it difficult to ignore your phone when you get a message, although you know it will harm your productivity.

Maybe you have a bad habit of eating junk food even though you know it's bad for your health. Perhaps you spend too much time checking your social media profiles even though you know doing so slows down the momentum you need to power through your to-do list. You can't control your urges if you don't know what they are. Therefore, make a list of them so that you can confront them head-on.

Step 2 - Write Out Your Goals: What are your short, medium, and long-term goals? Write them down and keep them in a location where you will see them every day so that you are constantly reminded of the things that are important to you. The decision to surrender to impulses is often made without thinking, but when your goals are always in front of you, they will cause you to think before you act, and over time, you will begin choosing to delay gratification.

Step 3 - Start Small: It takes time to overcome this negative habit, but as you take small steps, you will eventually have complete control over it. For example, if you have a habit of responding to texts and emails as soon as they come through, start by delaying your response time for 15 minutes for the first week. Increase the delay to 30 minutes during the following week, then 60 minutes the next week, and so on. This will help you develop self-control; it will also send a message to your brain that your urges don't control you and you can restrain yourself.

Step 4 - Take Pleasure in Resisting Your Urges: There is an empowering feeling associated with self-discipline. When you know you have control over your urges, the sky is the limit! When it comes to achieving your goals, self-discipline is more important than anything else because, without it, you won't take action.

Step 5 - Identify The Reasons Why You Seek Instant Gratification: What are the reasons you are always caving in to instant gratification? Do you feel more inclined to spend hours in front of the TV when you are stressed out? Do you drink too much when you are around certain friends or when you go to nightclubs? Once you have identified the factors that contribute to your negative behavior, avoid them until you are strong enough to control your urges.

Step 6 - Forgive Yourself: As I have mentioned, you are not going to conquer this problem overnight. Therefore, don't be too hard on yourself when you slip up. There will be times when you give into your urges no matter how hard you try; don't beat yourself up over it. Recognize that you are going to have the occasional stumble and keep moving forward. Everyone makes mistakes, and it hinders your productivity when you dwell on them.

TIP 12: STOP WAITING FOR THE RIGHT TIME TO ACT

When was the last time you said, "Now is not a good time." Whether you realize it or not, this phrase is often used as an excuse not to take action. For example, let's say you want to climb up the career ladder, and let's also imagine that doing so will require that you look for a new job with another company.

As a delay tactic, you might tell yourself, *"Now is not a good time,"* and then come up with as many excuses as you can to justify that statement. These excuses give you the permission you need to not take action.

Or, maybe you decide that alongside your full-time job, you want to start a side business so you can earn additional income. You never know, this idea may allow you to quit your full-time job. However, starting a business takes a lot of effort, and when you think about the things you will need to do to get going, you decide, *"Now is not a good time."*

It might seem sensible to wait until everything is in alignment before you take action, but the reality is that there is no such thing as the perfect time to act. There is always going to be an obstacle, a challenge, or a circumstance discouraging you from moving forward. The reality is that waiting for the perfect timing is a form of procrastination.

HOW WAITING FOR THE RIGHT TIME TO ACT ENCOURAGES PROCRASTINATION

First, waiting makes us complacent; it trains us to become comfortable with our current circumstances. We gain pleasure from thinking about our past achievements, which makes us feel that we don't need to keep pushing. For example, if you work in sales, you may have exceeded last month's sales goals and so feel that you don't need to put in the extra work required to reach them this month.

A college student might be so happy with their recent exam performance that they don't feel they need to study as hard for upcoming exams. Complacency not only puts limits on our productivity, but it also has a negative effect on our professional and personal growth.

Second, waiting for the perfect time to act results in missed opportunities. It trains us to believe that opportunities are occasions where we stand to benefit without risk. We adopt the mindset that all we need to do to take advantage of the opportunities is to accept them. But life doesn't work like that. Opportunities are not lottery tickets—they are accompanied by risk, risk of time wasted, risk of failure, etc. Refusing to accept such risk as a condition of pursuing opportunities is the same as refusing to pursue them altogether.

Third, waiting puts our goals on perpetual hold. Because circumstances never align perfectly, waiting or the perfect time to act essentially means we never take action. Consequently, we fail to achieve our goals, all of which require us to take purposeful action.

Action Steps

If you have fallen into the habit of waiting for circumstances to be perfect before taking action, now is the time to make a change, here are some steps to get you started:

Step 1 - Perfection Doesn't Exist: There is no such thing as the perfect time to act, there is always going to be something that could stop you from moving forward. The key is to work around your obstacles. Regardless of the forces hindering you, get started anyway.

Step 2 - Get Uncomfortable with Complacency: There is nothing wrong with being happy with where you are in life. However, if you know there is more you want to achieve, complacency isn't going to get you there. Continuous improvement should be your goal as it will ensure long-term happiness. The problem is that the brain prefers the status quo, so expect to encounter internal resistance when you start pursuing self-improvement. One way to break out of the status quo is to take on new challenges whenever they present themselves to you.

Step 3 - Take Small Steps: Even when circumstances are less than ideal, take small steps toward your goals. In doing so, you will desensitize your brain to the risk of taking action when things don't appear to be working out in your favor. For example, let's say you are waiting for the perfect time to pitch a potential client—don't wait, just pick up the phone and make your pitch.

The worst thing that can happen is the potential client will say no. Or maybe you are waiting for the perfect time to take your significant other on vacation—stop waiting, book the trip and go enjoy yourself! Again, what's the worst that can happen? By taking small steps, you are training the brain to recognize that intentions are only valuable if you are willing to take action to fulfill them.

Step 4 - Increase the Stakes: Developing the habit of taking action despite imperfect circumstances is like developing a muscle. Repetition and resistance are crucial. The more you exercise the habit, and the more resistance you overcome in doing so, the stronger the habit becomes. In the last step, you took small actions to desensitize yourself from the risks associated with acting without waiting.

In this step, take progressively larger actions, those that lead to bigger potential rewards, but also carry bigger risks. For example, start applying for the new job that will boost your career, launch the side business you've been contemplating for the past year. If you have been considering buying a new house, call a real estate agent to put your house on the market. Bigger actions equal bigger potential rewards. This is an essential part of accepting that waiting for the perfect moment to act only prevents you from moving forward.

Tip 13: Stop Using Productivity Apps

New productivity tools are EVIL! Yes, that's right, EVIL! Ironically, the things that claim to make you more productive can actually make you less productive. Why do I say this? All productivity tools promise to make you more efficient and effective by helping you to get more stuff done in less time. If you are anything like me, you are always seeking new ways to improve your productivity and it's easy to feel as if you are losing out if you don't at least try one of the tools you've seen advertised, even though you are already using a productivity tool that serves the same purpose.

For example, I have always used Google Calendar, it's easy to use and it's free. However, any time a new calendar app comes out, I have this urge to try it out. Eventually, I'm using three or four calendar apps at the same time, which is a complete waste of time! How ironic is that? I used to do the same thing with note-taking apps; when a new one came out, I'd get tempted again and the cycle would repeat itself. The problem is that we end up maintaining several productivity apps, many of which share the same features, and the end result is a drain on our productivity.

How Using Multiple Productivity Apps Encourages Procrastination

First, it causes confusion. For example, let's say you are using one app to keep track of your household maintenance such as bills, chores, different workflows, etc. You then decide to start using a note-taking app to make notes about travel plans, business ideas, and household expenses. Your friend then tells you about the great productivity app she's using and now you want to try that out. You keep this up until one day, you've got to find some important information, but you can't remember which app you used to made the notes. You've now got to waste time going through all your apps to find what you are looking for!

Second, using too many productivity apps opens the door to distraction. When you get something new, you want to play with it, so you can sit down for hours going through the different tools and features, and before you know it, you haven't checked off anything on your to-do list. We justify such time-wasting activities by convincing ourselves that they are going to improve our productivity when the reality is that we have allowed the app to become another time-wasting distraction.

Third, rushing to purchase every new productivity app trains us to believe that it's the apps that are responsible for our productivity and we tell ourselves that we wouldn't be able to get anything done without them. Productivity apps are supposed to be tools to optimize and streamline your current processes, and if you don't already have these processes in place, the apps are pointless.

ACTION STEPS

Productivity apps do not enhance our productivity. Productivity is a habit, and if you don't have the self-discipline to get things done throughout the day, the most powerful app in the world is not going to help you. If you have become trapped in the vicious cycle of using productivity apps, here are some steps to set you free:

Step 1 - Use One App Only: Don't get me wrong, I am in no way suggesting that you shouldn't use productivity apps. Just choose one—when I realized this, it made my life a whole lot easier.

Step 2 – Take Inventory of the Productivity Apps You Are Currently Using: Write down the apps you've installed on your browser, your phone, and the paper apps you are using. Work out which ones you use most often. If you are using more than one app per purpose, do you have a good reason for doing so? For example, does one of the apps have certain features that the others don't? Is one app easier to use than the other?

Step 3 - Combine Your Productivity Tools: If you are using multiple apps for one purpose, take note of the features that are most important to you, choose the one that has the majority of them and abandon the rest.

Step 4 - Stop Paying Attention to New Productivity Tools: Don't read any reviews or test any new productivity apps, because that will only entice you to purchase it and start using it. To overcome the temptation, don't indulge in it, not even for a second.

Step 4 - Use Apps That Work Together: This will help you streamline your processes and see your days, weeks, and months from a larger perspective. For example, I use Todist to maintain my to-do lists. This tool syncs with Google calendar, the integration of these tools allows me to automatically add events on my calendar to my Todist dashboard, and vice versa.

Tip 14: Start Writing Things Down Immediately

I used to have a bad habit of keeping my to-do lists in my head—I would rarely write anything down. There were times when I had a deadline and I would either only remember once the deadline had expired or remember on the day that the project was due. I would miss a lot of important appointments and meetings because of this bad habit, or do my grocery shopping and forget certain items and end up having to go all the way back to the store to get them. The brain possesses working memory to store information for short-term processing. But this resource is limited—unless it is recorded, you will forget many of the things you need to do.

That's the main aim of a to-do list— allowing you to get all the tasks and projects you need to complete out of your head and in writing so that you don't have to remember them. Not only does this free up your working memory, but it helps to ensure that items don't fall through the cracks. You might not like using productivity tools; in that case, keep a notepad and write things down on paper as you need to. With a proper task management system in place, you can have the confidence that your time and attention are spent where they will have the greatest impact.

Even if you are tempted to rely on memory only sometimes, don't do it. Committing miscellaneous items to memory such as dates and phone numbers might seem like a good idea because it appears you are saving time when you don't write them down. But in the long run, you will find that it ruins your productivity.

How a Failure to Write Things Down Encourages Procrastination

I have mentioned that when we fail to write things down, it is inevitable that certain items on our to-do list will fall through the cracks because the brain's working memory is not efficient enough to remember every last detail we need to track. After a while, we will start forgetting things, which can have a negative effect on our lives.

Keeping things in your head can make you feel overwhelmed. Most of us are juggling several tasks, projects, and responsibilities. Some carry terrible consequences if they are not completed, while others have deadlines, so it's easy to become overwhelmed when you are constantly trying to remember all the things you need to do.

Relying on your memory also makes it difficult to prioritize to-do items—it's hard enough to try to remember all the things you need to do let alone in what order.

When you fail to write things down, it also makes you more vulnerable to distraction. All the information in your head takes away from your ability to focus as trivial items creep in and take your attention away from the most important things. It makes concentration difficult and prevents you from entering a state of flow, in which you would otherwise experience a high level of productivity and performance.

Action Steps

If maintaining a to-do list is not something you are used to, it may seem difficult, but as soon as you start putting the habit into practice, you will begin to realize how effective it is. Below is a quick action plan to help you develop the habit of writing to-do lists.

Step 1 - Decide How You Are Going to Maintain Your To-do Lists: Whether you are going to write everything down on paper or use a productivity app, the first step is to decide how you are going to maintain your to-do lists. You might try an app and then decide you'd rather write things down in a notepad or vice versa.

Step 2 - Spend 10 Minutes per Day Writing Down the Things You Need to Do: Write them all down in one list, and don't worry about prioritizing them at this stage. Choose a time of day that works best for you. I prefer the evenings because it helps me remember the things I've got to do for the next day. You might prefer doing it first thing in the morning or the afternoon.

Step 3 - Highlight the Most Important Items: Once you have developed your list, highlight the things that demand urgent attention, and then assign them to a daily to-do list.

Step 4 - Put a Limit on Your To-do List: Shorter lists improve your motivation and focus. Ideally, you should have about seven items on your daily list. However, if you have a busy day, this might not work for you, but try not to have more than ten items on your list.

Step 5 - Keep Task Lists: As well as your daily to-do list, maintain a list of everything you need to do in the future. These items might include buying birthday cards or presents, taking your vehicle in for service, calling your parents, paying the bills, mowing the lawn, completing your weekly sales report, etc. You can also keep lists per project. For example, if you are writing a book, you might have a list that includes tasks such as: hire a cover designer, contact my agent, contact my editor, etc.

Step 6 – Prioritize: Use the 1-2-3 or A-B-C method to indicate the items on your lists that are of most importance, and then get those tasks completed first.

Tip 15: Apply the Two-Minute Rule

The majority of tasks we procrastinate over are relatively simple. We have the skills, talent, and abilities to get them done but for whatever reason, we keep avoiding them.

How Failure to Apply the Two-Minute Rule Encourages Procrastination

Procrastination is about doing everything else other than the things that are essential to achieving our end goal. When we don't apply the two-minute rule, those seemingly small tasks pile up, and when we finally get around to doing them it can take the entire day. We, therefore, end up having to push back other important tasks to get the things done we should have accomplished beforehand.

Action Steps

If you find you are constantly pushing back small tasks that take less than two minutes to complete, follow these steps to help you crush procrastination in this area.

Step 1 – Does it Take Less Than 2 Minutes? Do you have a stack of junk mail sitting on your desk, a pile of unfolded laundry on the couch, or a load of Amazon boxes decorating your bedroom? Work out the tasks you need to do that take less than two minutes and do them immediately.

Step 2 - Apply the Two-Minute Rule to All Goals: As I have mentioned, one of the reasons people fail to get things done is because they feel overwhelmed by the magnitude of the task. However, physics tells us that we are more likely to achieve our goals if we get started. Many years ago, Sir Isaac Newton taught us about the First Law of Motion, which stipulates that when a physical object is at rest, it stays at rest, and when it is in motion, it stays in motion.

This is why I don't agree that adults, other than the elderly, should take naps during the day. When I first started working as a freelancer, I had a desk in my bedroom, and by 3 pm I felt tired. Some experts believe that taking a 20-minute nap in the afternoon recharges your batteries, so I tried this out and found that it did the complete opposite and hindered my productivity. My 20-minute nap would turn into a two-hour nap, and by the time I woke up it was time for dinner. After dinner, my willpower was completely depleted, and I would spend the rest of the evening doing things that didn't require any energy like watch TV!

This went on for months until I was asked to work on a project about boosting productivity, and it was during this time that I realized what I was doing wrong. Again, whatever is in motion stays in motion, so now when I start feeling tired, I make myself some coffee and go for a 20-minute walk instead of taking a 20-minute nap. By the time I get back I'm ready to rock and roll!

Whatever habit you want to implement in your life, you can do so by applying the two-minute rule. Get moving to stay in motion, right? Therefore, if you want to get into the habit of reading, set a timer for two minutes per day and read the book of your choice. You will find that once that timer goes off you will want to continue, and before you know it, you've read an entire chapter or more. Do you want to start running every day? Get your gear on and go running for two minutes, and that two minutes will turn into 10 minutes or longer.

CONCLUSION

Procrastination is fun—taking part in leisure activities when you should be working on your goals or deadlines is enjoyable for the moment, until the stress and anxiety of not completing your tasks hits you.

As you have read, there is much more to procrastination than not getting things done. When you procrastinate calling your creditors to work out a payment plan, it affects your credit and you end up in debt. If you have a family, your debt will have a negative impact on other people's lives. If you procrastinate about changing your diet and getting into the habit of exercise, it will eventually affect your health.

Wisdom is the application of knowledge. I have provided you with the knowledge, now it's your responsibility to apply it. Procrastination plays a role even when we're storing up knowledge by reading book after book, going to different seminars, and watching videos. We convince ourselves that we are learning lessons we can apply to our lives, but in reality, we are still learning so we can put off applying those lessons. You will never know everything about any particular subject because knowledge is always evolving. Therefore, it's important to start applying what you already know if you want your life to change.

Now that you have read this book, get started on one of the tips in Chapter 11 before you start reading another book about procrastination. As I have mentioned, there is nothing wrong with continuous learning, but there is something wrong with storing up endless amounts of knowledge without applying any of it.

I can say with confidence that it is possible to beat procrastination if you are willing to put the work in. However, it is also important to understand that you are not going to become the king or queen of productivity overnight. Procrastination is a bad habit, and bad habits are difficult to break. Most people have been procrastinating their entire lives, so it is going to take a disciplined and focused effort to eliminate it.

Don't be too hard on yourself. If you fall, pick yourself up and try again. Remember, if babies gave up every time they fell when they were first learning to walk, the entire world would be still crawling! With every attempt to blast through procrastination, you are strengthening your resolve, and eventually, you will mount up on wings like an eagle and soar!

I wish you every success on your journey to overcoming procrastination!

THANKS FOR READING!

I really hope you enjoyed this book and, most of all, got more value from it than you had to give.

It would mean a lot to me if you left an Amazon review—I will reply to all questions asked!

Please visit www.pristinepublish.com/danielreview to leave your review.

Be sure to check out my email list, where I am constantly adding tons of value. The best way to get on the list currently is by visiting www.pristinepublish.com/morningbonus and entering your email.

Here I'll provide actionable information that aims to improve your enjoyment of life. I'll update you on my latest books, and I'll even send free e-books that I think you'll find useful.

Kindest regards,

Daniel Walter

ALSO BY

Daniel Walter

Discover how you can easily master focus and productivity to uplevel
your life in ways you never expected.

Visit: www.pristinepublish.com/daniel

REFERENCES

Burka, J. B., & Yuen, L. M. (2008). *Procrastination: Why You Do It, What to Do About It Now (2nd ed.). Amsterdam, Netherlands: Adfo Books.*

Collins, J., & Hansen, M. T. (2011). *Great by Choice.* New York, United States: Penguin Random House.

Corley, T. (2016). *Change Your Habits, Change Your Life: Strategies that Transformed 177 Average People into Self-Made Millionaires.* Amsterdam, Netherlands: Adfo Books.

Duckworth, A. (2020). *Grit: Why passion and resilience are the secrets to success.* New York, United States: Penguin.

Dweck, C. (2017). *Mindset - Updated Edition: Changing the Way You think To Fulfil Your Potential* (6th ed.). New York, United States: Robinson.

Ferrari, J. R. (2010). *Still Procrastinating.* Hoboken, NJ, United States: Wiley.

Fogg, B. (2019). *Tiny Habits: The Small Changes That Change Everything.* Amsterdam, Netherlands: Adfo Books.

Moore, R. (2016). *Life Leverage: How to Get More Done in Less Time, Outsource Everything & Create Your Ideal Mobile Lifestyle.* New York, United States: Macmillan Publishers.

Moore, R. (2018). *Start Now Get Perfect Later.* New York, USA: Nicholas Brealey.

Samuel, M., & Chiche, S. (2004). *The Power of Personal Accountability: Achieve What Matters to You.* Amsterdam, Netherlands: Amsterdam University Press.

Ziegler, D. (2002). *The Best Darn Book about Nutrition and Health.* Zaltbommel, Netherlands: Van Haren Publishing.